Your Resume

Sucks!

Your Resume **Sucks!**

The 3 Keys to a
Successful Resume

By

Mark Simon

Jeanne Simon

Dr. James E. M. Irvine, D.M

What others have to say about *Your Resume Sucks!* and lectures about resume writing given by Mark Simon

"Mark Simon's rock-solid resume building technique was a complete eye-opening experience for me. The common sense of it all will definitely have you wondering why you didn't think of it before. Whether you're the kid fresh out of school or the veteran business executive, this book is undeniably a must-have for today's working man!"

Christopher Boyd

"Mark's presentation is the kind that makes you snap your fingers and say 'That's so obvious, why didn't I think of that?'"

Mary Beason

"I've had 4 years at a university and 3 years Post Grad work, and I've learned more from your lectures in 2 evenings."

Tom Begley

"Thank you both (Mark & Jeanne) for everything you have done for me. I wouldn't be where I am now if it wasn't for you."

Bill George

"I thank you for all the things you taught through your book."

Babak Marjan

"Your ability to take what could have been a 'high-tech' subject of overwhelming 'buzz-words' and make it a clear, concise sharing of what's, why's and how's that we 'business folk' could understand was superb. We were all attentive to every word and found it a wonderful blend of education and entertainment."

Gene Romagna

"I wanted to take a moment and tell you that your resume (Mark Simon's) is very powerful and impressive."

Anthony L. Lopez

"I took your advice on resume-writing from Animation Magazine and it's a definite improvement."

Scott Peterson

"He knew exactly what he was doing and got that across to us with his experience."

Michelle Leach

"You guys rock! Thanks!"

Jack B.

If you are having a hard time getting job interviews, our resume writing system will get your resume noticed and get it put in the interview pile.

If you want a resume that works for you instead of the employer…This book is for you.

The Resume Rebels

Forward

With so many resume books out on the market, why write another? We wrote this book because what we suggest, works! Most of what's taught in schools by teachers and suggested by career counselors and well-meaning parents is not practical nor will it help you get an interview.

All the information in this book is based on our, the authors', combined 75+ years of experience. We will show you how to create the most dynamic possible presentation on paper as well as what information not to include on your resume that recruiters use to screen you out of the running. Many will initially disagree with the contents of this book, but after you finish reading it, you'll wonder why you wrote your resume any other way.

We know what a resume has to say and how to say it to get an interview. We know what makes a good resume because we've been freelancers for 50+ years and during that time we've applied for countless jobs and learned quickly what worked and what didn't. Conversely, as business owners, we've hired many others on the strength of their resumes and we've become quite adept at picking out effective employees from their resumes. Mark has also shared his knowledge through a series of lectures he's given to schools and professional groups regarding freelancing and career development.

Jeanne Simon's career spans over 30 years and she's also gotten freelance and staff jobs with her resume using our method. As a television producer, she reviewed hundreds of resumes a year and became proficient at quickly sizing up candidates from their resumes.

Dr. James E. M. Irvine, D.M., started his career over 30 years ago. His first resume out of college did not help him as he looked for his perfect job for over 2 years. Using our system of The 3 Keys to a Successful Resume, Jim quickly got interviews using his new resume and landed the job he was looking for within weeks. He now holds a Doctorate of Management in Organizational Leadership and works as a Human Resource specialist for Nissan North America. He has provided us with invaluable insight into large corporate hiring practices as well as researching the supporting evidence for our Keys.

We've used the form of a short story to illustrate our resume concepts for two reasons. One, most resume books are boring and no one reads them cover to cover, thus important concepts are missed. Two, people learn more when the subject is relevant and entertaining. Most everyone has gone on a job search and our story allows you to experience important resume feedback in a context that should be somewhat familiar. The examples used in this text are either based on actual events that happened to us or that we found in our research. Names were changed to protect the oblivious.

The back of this book is filled with supporting evidence and resume examples. In the resume section, you will find original resumes with explanations about what's wrong with them followed by revised resumes with a brief description of what was changed and why. The sample resume portion allows you to visualize the concepts we talk about in our story.

Our system, The 3 Keys to a Successful Resume, has worked time after time for professionals in a variety of careers and it will work for you too.

We are all proud when we can help someone succeed and get the job they want and deserve.

Now go get that job!

Mark & Jeanne Simon
Resume Rebels

Forward

A resume is a work of art. And like all art, beauty is in the eye of the beholder. The issue is who is 'beholding' your resume and do they see it as 'beautiful.' If there is a 'right' way or a 'wrong' way to write a resume, I'm not really that interested in it. What does interest me is what works. Academic and theoretical debates are boring…results are energizing.

I have spent hundreds of hours researching, discussing, and debating the 'correctness' of formats, fonts, and punctuation. Likewise, I have spent thousands of hours with 'real-live' managers reviewing resumes and making interviewing and hiring decisions based on our impressions of resumes like yours. You may not agree with the ideas or suggestions contained in this book, and that doesn't bother us a bit. However, the concepts contained in this book have, do, and will work. For many, the issue often boils down to the question: Do you want to be 'right' or do you want to be 'effective?'

The goal of this book is not to make you right, but to make you 'effective.'

James E. M. Irvine, D.M.

Table of Contents

THE FIRST KEY
Resume Header

A young man enters a contemporary office and approaches the secretary. He tells her, "I have a 9:30 appointment to see the owner of the company. I'm here to go over my resume with him."

She looks at the young man and smiles. "Well, I guess you're ready to open a few new doors in your life. He's been a mentor to a lot of young people in the past who now have very successful careers."

The young man smiles, takes a seat and looks around the well-appointed waiting room. He's impressed by the obviously expensive art hanging on the walls as well as numerous awards. His Dad's friend is the owner of this business and the young man knows that his Dad pulled a big favor getting him an appointment. Several groups of people pass through the waiting room. Some are dressed in suits while others are dressed in jeans and brightly-colored shirts.

The young man muses, "I wonder if my name will ever be hanging on the outside of a place like this." He shakes his head. "Not if I can't even get an interview it won't."

The secretary ushers the young man into a large office and an athletic man in his late 40's greets him with a warm smile and an outstretched hand. "How are you doing? Your Dad said you could use a few pointers on getting your next job."

The young man takes a seat and replies with a degree of frustration. "I've sent out at least 20 resumes in the last four months and not one person has called me. What's wrong with people? I mean...that seems so rude."

The executive suppresses a laugh and says, "Well let me take a look at your resume and see if we can figure out what's going on."

The executive studies the resume for what seems half a second and says, "The first problem is obvious. Whoever is looking at your resume has no idea what you do or what you want to do. You need to put a job title at the top of your resume."

The young man questions, "But how should I know what title to put? Shouldn't the person who's hiring decide what job I should have?"

The boss explains, "That's your job, not theirs. The people to whom you're sending your resumes probably receive hundreds of resumes for any number of positions*[1]. Recruiters and managers are typically short on time and attention*[2]. They need to know what you do with a quick glance at your resume*[3]. If it takes them more than a few seconds for them to figure out what you do, then your resume is used for trash can basketball."

"What if I've never done the job that I want, but it's my next step?" asks the young man.

"Your resume needs to support the job title at the top, whether you've actually done the job or not." The boss states bluntly.

A glimmer of understanding sweeps over the young man's face. "Well how would I know what to put for a job title?"

The executive replies, "Research. Call the recruiter, get online, or talk to someone who works at that company and find out exactly what positions they're hiring. Pick one that suits you and your experience and put that title boldly at the top of your resume. In fact, the job title and your telephone number are even more important than your name. Companies are seldom looking to hire a 'Sharon' or a 'Richard.' They're looking for an 'accountant' or 'salesman.'"

The young man looks confused. "I thought that my name and stating my objective were the most important things to have at the top of the resume." He thinks to himself, "At least that's what that one career coach told me."

The boss shakes his head. "Maybe it would be less

confusing if you think of a resume in parts and for our analogy we'll call the different parts 'keys.' I like to divide a resume into three main keys: Header, Experience, and Supporting Evidence. The First Key of your resume is the Header. The Header Key needs to fit the lock that opens the door to you getting an interview. The header should state the job title (the job you want), your name, phone numbers, a personal website if you have one, and an e-mail address. And since your resume will no doubt be e-mailed during your job search, keep in mind that the top third of your resume is what people will likely see on their computer monitors*[4]. It needs to be clear, concise and compelling enough to get people to scroll down."

The young man adds enthusiastically, "So I really need to come up with a great objective statement for the first key so people will want to see more." He reads from his resume, "My objective is to be a useful, well-paid employee..."

The executive interrupts him, "That's enough of that. I know a lot people will disagree with me, but I couldn't care less what your objective statement says. The fact that I received a resume from you tells me that your objective is to get a job and the job title tells me what you want to do. Once I know what job you want, then I look over the rest of your resume to see if your experience fits *my* needs. The bottom line is that when I am hiring for a position, I don't care much what the applicant *wants* from me, I am only interested in what they can *do* for me. Let's be honest, all objective statements really mean the same thing beneath all the mumbo jumbo and that is 'I want a job.'"

---

*All duh-jective statements really
mean the same thing:
I want a job.*

The young man laughs, "Hey. You know, you're right. Could I put that on my resume?"

The executive shakes his head no and replies, "You'd probably get points for honesty, but I wouldn't recommend it."

The young man gets serious and continues, "Well then how do I make my resume stand out?"

The executive replies, "By branding yourself. Think of yourself as the product; your resume as the commercial; and the employer as the consumer. Your resume has about three seconds to grab the attention of the consumer just like a commercial on TV has seconds to grab your attention and get you motivated to buy the product. Let's do a test. Match the company to this slogan…You're in good hands with…"

"Allstate," the young man continues. "Wait, wait, here's one…31 Flavors…Baskin Robbins."

The boss continues, "Good one, so you can see that in a few words, companies convey everything they want you to think and feel about them."

"Okay, I get that, but how do I come up with a statement like that for my resume?"

The executive turns to his desk and picks up a piece of paper. "It just so happens that I set aside a resume with a terrific example of branding. The job title reads 'Graphic Designer' and the line under it says, 'Fifteen years experience designing for Fortune 500 companies.' So, do you want to know more about this guy?"

The young man laughs, "I want to know more about this guy and I don't even want to hire him. He sounds like he knows what he's doing."

"Exactly, in seven words he's told you that he's a seasoned professional and that his work is in demand by some of the top companies in the world. Now let's look at your resume and come up with a branding line for you. Keep in mind that unlike most advertising, the statement you choose should be verifiable and not a subjective statement like 'I'm reliable and a people person blah, blah, blah.' Let's say your job title is Sales Executive and you should support that with something relevant. Have you won any awards or consistently met or exceeded sales quotas?"

The young man shakes his head no. "I've been in sales for three years. I was ranked in the top five sales people for the last two years. This year I made it to number two."

"I think we can work with that." The boss taps his head in thought, "How about Sales Executive? Top ranked professional with over three years experience."

"Wow, well that sounds pretty good. What if I couldn't say something like that? I mean what if I was applying for my first job?"

The executive replies, "Well then you may not be able to come up with a branding statement. If you can't, then just do your research and use the job title that the company is looking to fill and that fits your interests and qualifications as well. Just having the right title and a resume that's well organized and easy to read should catch the attention of someone who's looking to fill a job."

At that moment the phone rings and the executive answers it. "Yes. Thank you. I'll be right there."

The executive extends his hand to the young man and they shake. "Well our meeting is over and we've just gone over the First Key. Ms. Finley is the human resources recruiter for my firm and she would be an excellent person to tell you all about the Second Key. I'll set up a meeting for you with her one week from today at the same time."

The young man replies, "Thank you for your time. I'm a little confused because some of what you said contradicts what I've been taught, but I'll go ahead and update my resume based on what you've told me. Plus, now I've got some research to do."

The young man leaves the office thinking about what kind of job he wants.

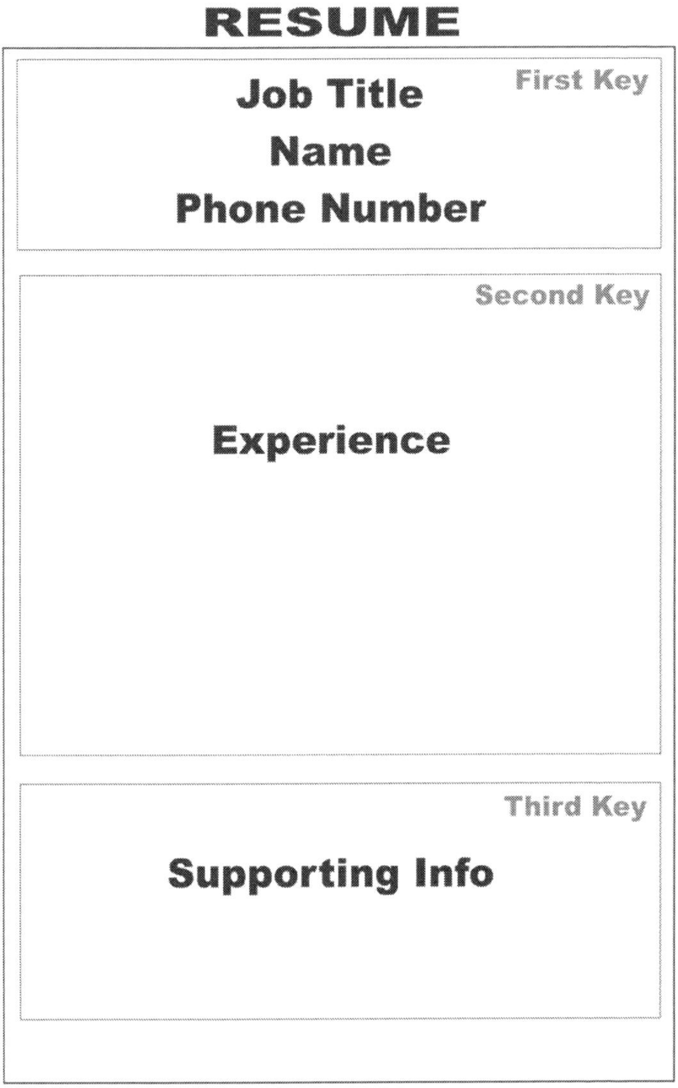

RESUME

Job Title   First Key

Name

Phone Number

Second Key

Experience

Third Key

Supporting Info

Figure 01

THE FIRST KEY
Resume Header

Job Title
- Clearly state the job title for which you are applying and if possible include a job code or job requisition number.
- The job title is more important than your name.
- Find out what jobs are available and customize your resume to the job that you are interested in and that your work history supports.

Objective Statement
- Do not include an objective statement. It is useless.
- Include a branding statement, if applicable, since it's a more powerful sales tool. State something positive and verifiable.
- Or, instead of a branding statement, if you have glowing remarks that someone made about your job performance in writing, put that on your resume.

Contact Information
- Make it large enough so even a bad fax machine won't make it unreadable.
- Don't use your current employer's phone number or your e-mail at work. Employers often track their employees' e-mail.

This Resume Sucks
Job Title

John Public
407-555-1234

Objective:
Seeking a position with a growing company where I may use my interpersonal skills and experience to help increase sales and moral company-wide.

Experience:
Shoes-2-Tight - Orlando, Fl
         Salesman of the Month four times in one year.

Clothing X-Pensive - Dallas, TX

Figure 02. Before

Figure 02 is typical of many of the resumes we've received. There is no job title, so recruiters and managers are left with the task of figuring out for what job John is applying. With possibly hundreds of other resumes to sift through, John's resume will most likely end up in the circular file.

The objective statement is also a waste of space and of the recruiter's time to read since they all say the same thing. When possible, objective statements should be replaced with a branding statement.

This Resume Rocks
Job Title

```
                    Salesperson
                    John Public
            Ranked #2 Salesperson Company Wide
                    407-555-1234

Experience:
Shoes-2-Tight - Orlando, Fl
        Salesman of the Month four times in one year.

Clothing X-Pensive - Dallas, TX
        * Sales
        * Display design
```

Figure 03. After

Figure 03 illustrates a heading that gets noticed. The clearly stated job title is in a prominent position which will be seen when flipping through a stack of resumes. Recruiters and managers seldom look to hire a John or a Cindy. They are looking for a salesperson or an accountant. It is not a recruiter's job to determine a job position for you. It is your job to tell her the position you wish to have and for which you're qualified.

In place of the duh-jective statement, John now has a branding statement, "Ranked #2 Salesperson Company Wide," which instantly differentiates him from other candidates. Of course, branding statements need to be true and verifiable. Not all resumes need or can justify a bold branding statement.

This Resume Sucks
Contact Information

John Public

Hometown, Georgia

Objective:
Seeking a position with a growing company where I may use my interpersonal skills and experience to help increase sales and moral company-wide.

Figure 04. Before

Notice how the drop-outs from the fax have made John's contact information almost unreadable. The last thing you want to have is a potential employer interested in interviewing you and not be able to call you.

Fax machines are not used as often as e-mail; however even printers can have dropouts at times. Plus, you never know if someone will fax your resume to someone else.

You're probably thinking, "No one would make their contact information so small." Oh, but they do and we've seen it done more than once.

This Resume Rocks
Contact Information

Salesperson
John Public
Ranked #2 Salesperson Company Wide
407 555 1234
jonpublic@awebsite.com
Hometown, Georgia

Figure 05. After

With the contact information in a larger point size, even a fax with drop-outs is still readable.

THE SECOND KEY
Resume Experience

One week later, the young man takes a seat in Ms. Finley's office and he smiles to himself because he's made all of the changes to his resume that the executive recommended. The young man is sure that Ms. Finley will have only glowing things to say about the rest of his resume.

A middle-aged, attractive women dressed professionally in a suit enters the office and extends her hand to the young man. She smiles warmly, "Good morning, I'm Ms. Finley and you must be the young man looking for a job. The boss told me all about you."

They both chuckle and sit down. The young man says, "You're right. I am looking for a job, but first I need to get an interview which apparently means that I needed to make some changes to my resume."

Ms. Finley says, "I know you've had at least one meeting with the boss and I'm sure that he had some suggestions."

The young man says, "Well, he had *lots* of suggestions, but one thing we didn't talk about was my cover letter. So I brought one to show you. Here's my revised resume and my cover letter."

He hands her the papers and she reads the cover letter first.

"Okay. Your cover letter is actually a great example of why the boss didn't address it in your first meeting. Cover letters usually don't convey information that is any different than the resume. We glance over them unless we need to fill a position that requires excellent written communication skills. When a possible candidate is identified and I e-mail that person's resume on to others for input, I rarely include the cover letter. "

The young man sighs, "I had the hardest time writing my

cover letter because I didn't know what to say that wasn't already in my resume. Are you saying that I don't need to include a cover letter?"

Ms. Finley answers, "Most of them all say the exact same thing so they're a waste of my time to read them. A friend of mine in the restaurant business fills as many as a hundred positions each summer season and says that he never reads cover letters because he doesn't want to know someone's life history; he just wants to know that a candidate has experience."

The young man adds, "And a resume has that information."

Ms. Finley continues, "Right. There are some exceptions, of course. If fewer than five people respond to a job posting, I may read the cover letters just to see if I can find some added bit of information to differentiate them. Or, as I mentioned earlier, some positions must be filled with someone who has exceptional writing skills. In these cases, cover letters can tell me a lot about the candidates. So, if you do decide to include a cover letter keep it short and professional. It should be typed with the addressee's name spelled correctly and it should be signed. If possible, include information which separates you from others that either isn't on the resume or that is on the resume, but is so abbreviated or outstanding that it bears further explanation."

The young man counters, "Can you give me an example?"

"Sure. Let's say you're applying for a job as an HR manager and you find out that the company looking to hire is researching new databases. You have a section listing software on your resume, but what isn't apparent is that you were involved in the search and implementation of your department's latest database. Further describing your database experience in a cover letter would give you an edge."

The young man says, "Let's say that I've been referred by someone for a job. I should put that in a cover letter, right?"

"Absolutely. There's really no place for that on a resume. Of course include the name of the person who referred you and his/her title, what your relationship is to the person referring you, and the job for which you're applying. It's also a good idea to do a little research and get a company-issued job description and briefly point out how your experience fulfills their requirements. Always, always, always ask for an interview and state a date when you will follow up with them and ask about a convenient time for a meeting. If you do those things in a cover letter it will definitely work to your advantage."

The young man sighs and smiles, "Okay everything you said makes sense. When I wrote this cover letter I felt like I was just repeating myself. So what do you think of my revised resume? I don't think there are too many other things to change."

Ms. Finley takes a moment to look over the resume then says, "I like the way you have the job title, your name and phone number at the top of your resume. However, the section where you list experience is confusing and I'll bet misleading. We need to work on your Second Resume Key."

"The boss mentioned the First Key last week," says the young man. "What's the Second Key?"

"The second key is where you include your relevant work experience," says Ms. Finley. "It's the key that will unlock the door to your job interview. Let's role play for a moment. I'll be interviewing you for a job and you be you."

The young man laughs, "Okay, I'll do my best."

The recruiter gets serious, "It looks as though you had a six month gap in between jobs. What were you doing during that time?"

The young man shrugs his shoulders, "Oh, I was helping my Mom in her stationery store. One of her employees was in a car accident and I had just been laid off so I gave her a hand."

Ms. Finley asks, "Why didn't you put that experience on your resume?"

The young man replies, "Well, I didn't get paid for that work and it was just for my Mom."

The recruiter follows up, "What did your duties include while you worked for her?"

The young man answers, "I worked the cash register and took inventory. I ordered items when supplies got low and I helped arrange product displays. Plus, I did a little accounting."

The recruiter says, "Okay, let's stop role playing for a moment and discuss your resume. First of all, you shouldn't include dates as part of your employment history."

The young man is shocked, "Wow! That's a surprise. My career counselor at school and even my Dad told me that I have to list dates for each job that I've had."

Ms. Finley explains, "Including dates for each job you've held may lead whoever is looking at your resume to draw some incorrect assumptions. Besides, the goal of your resume is to get you an interview. If the company is interested in you, the job application form may require dates and you can list them there."

The young man says, "Okay, but I'm not sure what you mean. How could dates be misleading? "

Ms. Finley says, "Any number of ways. For instance, when a recruiter sees a gap in dates she will usually think the worst."

The young man adds, "Like I was goofing off?"

The recruiter continues, "Precisely, or she might think that you were terminated and had a difficult time finding another job. Or who knows? The point is, dates might lead the recruiter to incorrect assumptions or they might give away your age. Whoever is doing the hiring often has in mind how old the ideal employee should be. Employers, for instance, have a tendency to hire someone close to their age or near the age that they were when they held the position that's now open*[5]. The employer may not be aware of her age preferences, but this sort of filtering is a subconscious part of human nature. Therefore, if you state your age or reveal it some other way and it's either older or younger than the image the recruiter has in mind, then she may consciously or unconsciously not consider you as the perfect candidate for the job. Unfair? Discriminatory? Yes, certainly, but then again you volunteered the information. If you don't make your age apparent, then whoever is considering you for the job is more likely to assume you are the perfect age*[6].

The young man asks, "But what happens when I show up for the interview and I'm older or younger than what the interviewer expects?"

The recruiter replies, "Just remember that the key function of the resume is to get you an interview. Think of it this way, if you get the interview, then your resume served its main purpose. Once you're in the door, it's time for you to sell yourself and get the job. If you sense that age is an issue, then prove otherwise by selling the advantages of your age. Make this a rule: *Don't include anything on your resume that could possibly work against you in getting an interview.*"

The young man shakes his head in disbelief. "I never realized how something as simple as dates could give away so much information that could possibly be a negative."

Seemingly harmless information, such as, graduation dates or the reason why you left a job could create a negative impression in the recruiter's mind.

Ms. Finley continues, "Now I'll give you an example of how *not* putting dates on a resume leads people to think the best. A friend of mine is a storyboard artist for film and TV. He lists the Adam Sandler film *The Waterboy* among his credits. He designed the team logo, a tattoo and drew all of the storyboards for the film. Most people who look at resumes for the film industry know that a film such as this one takes six or more months to complete. How long would you guess that my friend worked on *The Waterboy*?"

The young man answers, "Well I know this is a trick question. It sounds like he did a lot, so I'll guess at least three months."

The recruiter smiles, "No, he worked only three days! Now if he had put June 3-5 on his resume, what would you think?"

The young man hesitates, "Well...I'd think that what he did wasn't all that important or that maybe he got fired."

Ms. Finley agrees, "Exactly. You'd think negative things when that wasn't the case at all. My friend simply completed what the show needed in a short amount of time. His speed was actually an asset to the producers. By not putting dates on his resume he is allowing whoever is looking at the resume to form his own impression of how long the work should take. In most cases, a person looking at my friend's resume would be impressed that he worked on such a big movie and designed high-profile art for the film. They would also undoubtedly assume, as you did, that he worked much longer on the project than the actual three days. It is your job to create the most positive impression of yourself possible on paper while being truthful."

The young man says, "That was a great example. Do you have another one?"

The recruiter replies with a smile, "As a matter of fact I do and it's kind of a different one. A man in his late thirties, we'll call him Karl, applied for a job here not too long ago and put his graduation date from a college*[7] where he had just earned a second degree. An associate of mine scanned the resume quickly and assumed him to be a much younger person based on his graduation date and consequently missed the depth of experience he had gained prior to his second degree. His resume made it to my desk and after I studied it, I realized that we had an ideal candidate for a job opening and he got an interview."

The young man asks incredulously, "Are you saying we shouldn't put graduation dates on our resumes?"

Ms. Finley nods affirmatively, "That's exactly what I'm saying. What matters is that you have earned the degrees and not necessarily when you graduated. In the example that I just gave you, we were looking for someone who had years of solid work experience. Seeing such a recent graduation date threw us off since we thought Karl was much younger."

The young man asks, "What happens if I get asked in an interview about when I graduated or how long I held a job?"

Ms. Finley explains, "Those are reasonable questions that deserve an answer. Be honest and accurate. Chances are though that the recruiter will not ask you the dates for every job experience you list. The point is: don't volunteer any information that could be construed as negative in any way."

The young man replies, "Okay. I get it. No dates on my resume."

The recruiter adds, "Remember the purpose of your resume is to *get* you the interview, so your resume has done its job if you get that far. Answering detailed and specific questions is always part of an interview."

She continues, "Now, why did you feel the need to explain the reason you left your previous job on your resume?"

"I had been told that I always should," he explains. "Is that bad?"

"Absolutely," responds Ms. Finley. "Regardless of your answer, stating why you left any job leaves a slightly negative impression and reads like an excuse*[8]...even if you were laid off. Your resume should only celebrate the good things in your career. These days it's common for people to move from job to job*[9] in order to quickly build their careers."

Ms. Finley changes topics. "You said that you did not

include the experience of working in your mother's store because it was for her and you did not get paid. You should have definitely included this on your resume. Whether or not you were paid does not diminish the work you did or the knowledge that you gained*[10]. You should have included that job on your resume because it supports your career path."

The young man questions, "If I put it on my resume, then I should say that I volunteered my time, right?"

"No, don't do that." Ms Finley counters. "No one needs to know that you were not compensated with money. If you included that information most people would devalue the work you did. By treating that job as you would any other, a recruiter will assume that you got paid and give it the same value as your other work experience. Again that sort of information takes away from making the best impression possible, so don't include it."

The young man adds, "You know, now you've got me thinking about other things that I may need to add to my resume that I don't have on there now. I did an internship in my junior year that I wasn't paid for."

The recruiter adds, "Good idea. Just make sure that whatever you put on your resume is relevant to the job for which you're applying. In fact, why is your most relevant job experience listed third on your resume?"

The young man replies, "Because the first two were more recent. Wouldn't it be weird to put them out of order?"

"Not if you don't use dates," says Ms. Finley. "Your resume needs to emphasize that you are the right person for the job. Your experience should always start with your most relevant work history, not necessarily your most recent. This means that you may have several versions of your resume, because different jobs may make different experiences more relevant. Again, this requires you to research each job you apply for."

Don't list work history chronologically; instead, list experiences according to the degree to which they support the stated job title at the top of your resume beginning with that experience which most directly supports the title and listing the least supportive last.

The young man's eye light up. "I get it. Without dates, the order of my work experience probably won't even be questioned."

Ms. Finley responds, "That's right. Now let's keep role playing. I see that you were manager of a shoe store. That seems like a lot of responsibility so early on in your career."

The young man blushes, "Well, I wasn't officially *the* manager. The guy that held that job was such a slacker that I basically did his job and mine, so I put that I was the manager on my resume."

Ms. Finley asks, "So if I did some checking I would discover that you never actually held the manager job at the shoe store? I would find out that you were what? A sales person?"

The young man replies, "That's right."

The recruiter leans forward in her chair to emphasize her point. "We're not role playing right now. You may think that what you did was harmless. Lying on a resume about anything is a bad idea. Believe me it's just a matter of time before you're found out and lying on a resume is almost always considered a reason for termination. At our company, and many others, we always conduct extensive background and reference checks on everyone we hire*[11]. We can't afford not to. Lying on a resume is a one-strike-and-your-out offense."

The young man has a shocked look on his face. "How could someone ever find that out? I mean, it was so long ago and I really did do the work."

Ms. Finley says, "I'll give you two real examples of gentlemen who lied about their past and they got caught at it. This first young man, we'll call him Bill, was interviewing for a designer position with Matt, the creative director. Matt questioned Bill about a credit he had listed on his resume as designer on a project called *Girls in Space*. Bill confirmed that he had been the designer, but couldn't answer any specific questions about it. Matt let Bill squirm through two or three more questions then told Bill that he couldn't have been the designer on *Girls In Space* because that's the position that Matt had held."

The young man gasps, "Whoa! That was bad luck!"

Ms. Finley replies, "No, that was stupid. Not only did he lie, he didn't even research whose credit he had stolen. It's very easy to have thorough background checks done inexpensively and quickly*[12]. Here is another example about lying that is a little bit different. Tom worked in a corporate environment as a talent scout. He had an abrasive personality and a lot of his co-workers complained about him and his supervisor was looking for a reason to fire him. Tom's performance was satisfactory and he hadn't done anything to merit dismissal. Human resources did some routine checks and found that Tom had lied on his resume about his education. Tom had stated that he had an advanced degree when he really did not and the deception cost him his job."

The young man shakes his head, "I get it. I'll go over my resume carefully and make sure that everything on there can be backed up."

The recruiter says, "Good idea. On your resume you should list the title of shoe salesman and you may legitimately list the extra duties you performed and quantifiable results you achieved while you were in that position."

The young man questions, "I understand what you mean by listing duties, but what do you mean by listing results?"

The recruiter continues, "First let me clarify listing duties. In many instances, when you list a job title, the duties you performed are obvious. For example, as a shoe salesman you don't need to state that you fitted customers for shoes. That's a given. We call it the Duh Factor. Don't restate the obvious or it will seem that you don't know what you are talking about. In your particular case, what may not be so obvious is that you also tracked inventory and interviewed others for sales positions. You obviously had extra responsibility that should be noted. Results are even more important to put on your resume than duties. Let's say, that while you were a shoe salesperson that sales rose by 30% and returns declined by 20%. Maybe you were their number two salesperson and attained 145% of your quota. That's something that you should put on your resume. Recruiters are impressed by those who create and track positive results."

The young man says, "That's great, but not everyone is in sales so they don't have those kinds of results to put on their resumes. What are other ways you can communicate results?"

Ms. Finley replies, "In every job there is a measurement of success. For instance, a female friend of mine is producer of television shows and she's able to state on her resume that she has been nominated for several national broadcast awards. Any executive producer reading her resume would be impressed."

The young man nods in agreement, "You know, I have to think about it, but I think I can add some results to my resume. I can work on that for my next meeting with the boss as well as changing *most* of my resume."

They both laugh. The recruiter adds, "Well you do have some work to do, but it will make a huge difference. I guarantee it. There are really just a few more things you'll need to do to perfect your resume."

The young man says, "That sounds great. Thank you for all of your suggestions. I really appreciate it."

The young man leaves the recruiter's office and before he exits the building he sits in the waiting room and goes over the notes he took.

THE SECOND KEY
Resume Experience

Dates
- Do not list dates because they can give away your age and lead to incorrect and negative conclusions.

Job Departure
- Never list reasons for leaving a job because they always leave negative impressions and read like excuses.

Experience
- Include all relevant experiences - paid and unpaid.
- List the most relevant experience first, not the most recent.

Be Truthful
- Lying on a resume will catch up to you and could cost you your job.

List Results
- Employers hire others who produce results. Instead of an obvious job description, list concrete and verifiable results.

The Job Duh Factor
- Don't list duties which are obvious from job titles.

Extra Job Duties
- Highlight what you did above and beyond your job titles.

This Resume Sucks
Dates

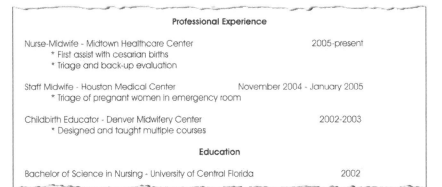

Professional Experience

Nurse-Midwife - Midtown Healthcare Center   2005-present
  * First assist with cesarian births
  * Triage and back-up evaluation

Staff Midwife - Houston Medical Center   November 2004 - January 2005
  * Triage of pregnant women in emergency room

Childbirth Educator - Denver Midwifery Center   2002-2003
  * Designed and taught multiple courses

Education

Bachelor of Science in Nursing - University of Central Florida   2002

Figure 06. Before

While the dates above may seem harmless, we make assumptions based on these dates that may be wrong.

Her second job listing indicates only three months employment. Your first assumption may be that she was let go and may not be very good at her job when perhaps what really happened was that she was so outstanding that she was either sought after by another facility or was transferred with a promotion from one facility to another.

We also see there is a gap in the dates between her second and third jobs. A typical assumption would be that she had trouble finding another position. That would also support our initial conclusion above. Perhaps she held a job not pertinent to her midwife career path and simply left out the interim job.

We see that she graduated four years ago if you are reading this in 2006. We would typically gauge her age to be between 22-25 years old based on her graduation year. The recruiter knows the job specs dictate that candidates must have at least 7 years experience in a hospital environment and a person just 25 years old couldn't meet the requirement. However, what if this person had gone back to school for her nursing degree and had spent years in hospitals in another capacity? Again, our assumptions could be wrong.

This Resume Rocks
Dates

Professional Experience

Nurse-Midwife - Midtown Healthcare Center
   * First assist with cesarian births
   * Triage and back-up evaluation

Staff Midwife - Houston Medical Center
   * Triage of pregnant women in emergency room

Childbirth Educator - Denver Midwifery Center
   * Designed and taught multiple courses

Education

Bachelor of Science in Nursing - University of Central Florida

Bachelor of Psychology - Miami University
   * Minor in Administration

Figure 07. After

We removed all of the dates which accomplish a few goals. First of all, it eliminates all of the possible negative assumptions as discussed on the previous page. The amount of time spent on a job or lapses in work are now not an issue.

Removing the dates offers her another option as well. Say she's applying for a position where her childbirth education experience is the most relevant. Without dates she can easily move that job to the top of her experience list since putting jobs out of chronological order is only a problem when using dates.

Without the graduation year, we have a much harder time determining her age. Also take note of her second degree which could have been earned two years earlier or ten years earlier.

Eliminating dates robs recruiters of one of their favorite screening tactics.

This Resume Sucks
'Duh Factor' and Lying

Career Path

Vice President Business Development - Union First Bank
    Increased new clientele by 120% in two years.
    Top sales performer in 2002, 2003.

Director of Expense Management - New York Capital
    Oversaw Expense Management team.
    Increased group performance by 110%.

Education

Master of Business Administration, University of Pennsylvania
Bachelor of Science in Accounting, Columbia University
    Major: Finance
    Major: Communications

Figure 08. Before

The Duh Factor is when a resume states the obvious. Under the job title, Director of Expense Management, he states "Oversaw Expense Management team." Of course that's what he did; he was the director of the department. Supporting job statements need to be items that are not obvious, such as his line on how much he improved group performance.

Lying on a resume is serious and reason for termination if it is found. We can look at two examples here. To prove a point, let's say that the resume writer did not hold the title of director of the department. The director was on administrative leave and he ran the department in her absence. This is valuable information to share with a recruiter, but you can't list a job title that you didn't officially hold.

Again, to illustrate a point, let's say that he's applying for a position that requires a degree in finance. He took a finance course at Columbia University and did well, so he stated that finance was one of his majors, when in fact it was not.

Either one of these lies, as minor as they seem, could get him fired or keep him from being hired in the first place.

This Resume Rocks
Duh Factor and Lying

Career Path

Vice President Business Development - Union First Bank
   Increased new clientele by 120% in two years.
   Top sales performer in 2002, 2003.

Senior Manager of Expense Management - New York Capital
   Ran department while Director was on administrative leave.
   Reduced expenses and headcount.
   Increased group performance by 110%.

Education

Master of Business Administration, University of Pennsylvania
Bachelor of Science in Accounting, Columbia University
   Major: Communications
   Course in Finance

Figure 9. After

The "Duh Factor" was easily eliminated by simply deleting any reference or job description that was obvious.

The job candidate was trying to take credit for work he actually did when he overstated his job title. However, it still wasn't completely true. The right way to handle that situation is to be direct and accurate. We now state his proper title and describe his role in running the department in his boss's absence.

The lie in his education section has been deleted and his education accurately stated.

Don't over-state or embellish your educational background. It's the most often checked and most easily verifiable part of a resume.

This Cover Letter Sucks

Evette Smith
Evette@somewebaddress.com
(555)123-4567

In the interest of seeking immediate employment opportunities within your organization, I have enclosed my resume for your review and consideration. It documents my experience, qualifications and accomplishments.

I am primarily interested in a position, which allows me to utilize my ten years of diverse experience. I feel that I can make immediate contributions to the goals and profits of your company.

Some of my attributes are my tenacity for getting the job done as well as being a team player. In addition, my personal work performance is one of dedication, commitment and the willingness to "go the extra mile". I am flexible in new situations and will perform according to the highest standards. My dedication and hands-on experience, supported by my education and interpersonal skills, make me an ideal candidate for undertaking any challenge within your organization.

Thank you for considering my credentials. I would appreciate an opportunity to discuss with you, in person, ways in which my background will assist your company in achieving its goals.

I look forward to hearing from you.

Sincerely,

Evette Smith

Enclosure

Figure 10

This Cover Letter Sucks

There is very little substance to Evette's cover letter which reads exactly like many others we've received. It also is not formatted correctly as it is missing the business name and address, date, and a salutation.

In the first paragraph, she says she sent her resume for review in order to get a job. Why else would someone send in a resume? Again, this is the "DUH" factor. It would have been somewhat acceptable if she had at least mentioned the job for which she was applying.

Evette continues to describe what a resume is: "It documents my experience, qualifications and accomplishments." Her statement is hopefully true about her resume, but since recruiters know the purpose of resumes, her statement seems like filler and it comes across as condescending and naive.

Her second paragraph contains the only bit of useful information in the entire letter. She tells us that she has ten years of work experience; however, she surrounds it with a wish for an uncertain job position and a bland, over-used statement that she can contribute to the company.

The third paragraph mentions being a team player, her dedication, going the extra mile and her flexibility with no supporting evidence. These are all characteristics listed by almost every candidate and should be assumed for every worker.

This Cover Letter Rocks

Evette Smith   Home: 222-222-222
101 South Street   Mobile: 222-222-2222
Orlando, Florida 332888   Evette@yahoo.com

June 26, 20XX

Mr. John Recruiter
Director of Human Resources
Company Q
123 North Front Street
Orlando, Florida 33333

Dear Mr. Recruiter;

I am writing about a position for an accounting manager that I saw advertised in the *Orlando Sentinel*. With the recent merger of Company Q with MegaCompany C, it appears that you need more accounting managers to handle the added work load and I'm confident in my ability to make an immediate and long-term contribution given the skills I've developed and contacts I've made as an accounting manager at Company X. As the following comparison shows, my experience and background come close to satisfying all the requirements stated in your ad.

Your Requirements	My Qualifications
College degree	B.S. in Accounting
Proven ability to manage accounts	Skilled at handling accounts through all stages of development
Ability to work within a team	Proven team leader

The enclosed resume will provide additional information about my qualifications.

I would very much appreciate the opportunity to meet with you and discuss the ways in which I can help Company X achieve its goals. I will call your office on July 1 to determine whether there is a convenient time for you to see me.

Sincerely,

Evette Smith
Enclosure

This Cover Letter Rocks

First of all, it's formatted correctly with the correct spelling of the recruiter's name and address of the company. Plus she has all of her contact information at the top of the letter just in case her resume gets lost.

In the first paragraph, Evette states why she is writing and the job for which she'd like to be considered. She also states how and why she can be an asset to the company. She also does something which is bound to impress any recruiter by referring to the recent merger of Company Q and MegaCompany C. This shows she's up on what's going on in her field and that she's done her homework. A big plus!

She also lists some of the requirements for the job as stated in the ad and shows how she's qualified.

In the last paragraph, Evette politely asks for an interview and gives the date when she'll follow up. Every cover letter should close in this way.

All the extraneous information has been removed.

THE THIRD KEY
Resume Supporting Evidence

The young man enters the executive's office anticipating congratulations on his revised resume.

The executive says, "Good morning!" as he holds up a faxed copy of the young man's resume. It's unreadable due to black lines and general darkness that obscures the image.

The young man says, "Wow. That looks terrible. Let me give you a clean copy on the original stationary."

The executive says, "Thank you. I'll take one, but you should always send yourself a test fax to see how your resume will be received. This is also true when e-mailing your resume. Well... I have more to say about your presentation, but I don't want to get ahead of myself. I can tell by your updated resume that Ms. Finley thoroughly covered the Second Key with you, so we should focus on the Third Key. Presentation, such as how poorly your faxed resume looks is part of polishing the keys and I'd like to cover that last."

The young man says, "After I learned about the first two keys, the Header and Experience, I changed my resume a lot. There's probably not much to change now."

The boss smiles, "I see a few things, but first let me explain what the Third Key is. The Third Key is supporting information. It's the key that will swing the door open for your interview."

The young man jumps in, "Oh I know, like where I went to school and what my hobbies are."

The executive says, "You're right and wrong. You're right about including education, but wrong about..." He points to the young man's resume "...including tennis."

The young man argues, "But doesn't that show that I'm a well-rounded athletic person?"

The executive explains, "It could, but it doesn't directly

or indirectly support the job title you've listed or the experience you've documented. I look at it and wonder why it's there? The job I'm hiring for doesn't require a killer back hand. It becomes a distraction and makes you look like an amateur in my eyes."

The young man questions, "An amateur?"

The boss continues, "Well, most successful professionals are laser in their focus and know exactly what information *not* to include on a resume. Typically the best resumes I get are from those who have been in the work place for three or more years and who know what it takes to get my attention and make my job easy. Every time I hire someone, I am entrusting them with my reputation. Past performance is a good predictor of future success. As with most rules though, there are exceptions. Let me give you two examples. If you were applying for a membership sales job at a tennis club, do you think that including playing tennis on your resume is relevant?"

The young man hesitates, "I think so..."

The executive answers, "Of course it would be. That small piece of information at the bottom of your resume could make the difference between you getting a call for an interview or another guy. Here's another example that's not so obvious. A male friend of mine who's around 60 was looking for a job last year. He didn't put on his resume how old he was or dates of any kind, but his age was clear to anyone by the depth of his experience and the types of projects he had worked on. He wasn't getting many interviews so he asked me to go over his resume with him. I concluded that even though he had excellent qualifications for the jobs for which he was applying, that he wasn't getting any calls because recruiters were reluctant to consider hiring someone in his sixties. After we talked a little he mentioned that he's never felt more physically fit or mentally alert in his life and he credited martial arts. At that time he had just earned his second degree black belt."

The young man says, "That's impressive and it takes a lot of dedication."

The boss continues, "You're right about that. I urged my friend to include some information about his martial arts training on his resume. He did and sent out a few more resumes. He got a call from the CEO of one of the companies to which he had sent his resume. The CEO happened to be a black belt himself and told my friend that anyone with his experience who had the kind of discipline and dedication it took to earn a second degree black belt would be welcome at his company. My friend was able to set up an interview with the CEO the following week and he started work the following month."

The young man says, "What a great story. It makes me want to take martial arts."

The boss says, "That's not the point. The point is that you must intentionally manage the reader's impression of you. You must know what about yourself to put on your resume that gives you an edge over every one else."

The young man says, "Well I can play the guitar...badly. I sang in the school choir?"

The boss just shakes his head no.

The young man adds, "I can speak Spanish."

The boss asks, "Do you speak Spanish fluently?"

The young man answers, "Yes. As a matter of fact, I was a foreign exchange student my senior year in high school. I stayed with a family in Barcelona. It was a great experience."

The boss claps his hands together, "Now we're getting somewhere. The ability to speak in two or more languages is always a plus and should absolutely be on your resume*[13]. Many times, a job posting will state that fluency, in say Spanish, is a pre-requisite for the job and in that case you should create a version of your resume that highlights your special talent."

Being multi-lingual almost always works to your advantage and should be included on your resume.

The young man asks, "What if it's not part of the job description?"

The executive answers, "Good question. It should go near the bottom of your resume along with your educational background and any awards you've won. Any professional associations you may belong to should also go in this section."

The young man says, "It sounds like the Third Key focuses on where you place the information that isn't included in the first two sections."

The executive says, "Well that's true, but its position on the resume doesn't diminish its importance. If some one is interested enough to read your entire resume what he sees last on the page could trigger him to call you for an interview. For instance, when I applied for my first sales job, my resume included an award I had won for debating in high school. The sales manager figured that I must be better than average at getting a point across so he called me to interview for a job."

He continues, "You should also delete this statement, 'I'm a people person.'"

"But, I like to think of myself as working well with others. Don't employers want that?" says the young man.

"Of course we do," says the executive. "But working with others should be a given, not a special talent. Whenever someone makes a statement like that, I tend to think the opposite is true and he is probably difficult to get along with. Besides, telling me you're a people person has little credibility.

Prove it to me through your results."

"Oh. Then I should probably also lose the statement about being a hard worker." The young man then questions, "Since the Third Key is a catch-all area of information, what order should it be put in? In other words, should education always be put first?"

Experience trumps education.

The executive replies, "Another good question! No, education shouldn't always be listed first in that section. Consider the information as a whole that you're including in the Third Key and list it in order of relevance to the job for which you're applying. Only put education first in the section if education is very important to the person doing the hiring. If you're applying for a sales job and you won Salesman of the Year it makes more sense to start off the Third Key with that rather than listing the college you attended."

The young man says, "Well that makes sense, but I'm still stuck on education and maybe that's because I was so recently in school. It seems like teachers and parents are constantly talking about how doing well in school and going to the right college will impact the kinds of jobs you can get and how much money you can make. Why shouldn't education and grade point average be among the main points on a resume?"

The executive explains, "The answer to that question is absolutely dependant on what sort of career path you are seeking. Let's say you attended Harvard Law School and you're applying for a position with a law firm. Where you received your degree gives you an edge over the competition, so you would most likely put that information first in the Third Key. Each profession considers certain universities as being the best in their field. If your education is from one of those schools or is particularly relevant or impressive, then it should be given special consideration and placement. Keep in mind though, as you advance in your career and gain experience and valuable contacts, your education will take a back seat to what you've done on the job. Your education may not matter at all in many creative fields. I have an artist friend who has a degree with two majors. Since he didn't go to one of the top schools in his field he's never listed his education on his resume. He's worked on over 2,000 projects and has never been asked if he graduated from a university. Clients were more interested in his talent and experience*[14]."

The young man says, "Well that's good to know. I went to a state university and I had about a 3.2 GPA."

The executive says, "That's fine, but don't put your GPA on your resume. I've seen resumes that list a 4.0 GPA. While yours is respectable, you instantly take a back seat to the person with the 4.0 GPA. If you don't list your GPA, you stay on equal footing. Remember, don't include any information if it could work against you. For instance, take this section on your resume where you list software. You state that you use CorelDraw 10 and WordPerfect 9."

The young man beams, "Yes I do. I try to stay current with the best software."

"Okay," says the executive. "However, we just updated to CorelDRAW 12 and the latest version of WordPerfect X3. By including the software version numbers, your skill level appears more and more dated with each software update.*[15]"

"Oh," says the young man. "But, I can always update the list."

The executive replies, "You can't update a delivered resume. If you leave off the version numbers, it will never look outdated. Oh, by the way, always double check the spelling of software. CorelDRAW is spelled with DRAW in all caps. Even if you think you know how to spell the software names, take a few seconds to look at the packaging or Google them and you'll get the correct spelling."

The young man adds, "That's a good tip. Do I need to list operating platforms?"

The executive shakes his head no. "It's not necessary because software is so compatible today and the platforms are not an indicator of skills. Okay let's wrap up our time this morning and discuss personal information. You shouldn't put personal facts like marital status, height or weight...."

The young man interrupts, "...Unless it could help me get the job."

"Yes. You give me an example this time," says the executive.

"Well," the young man responds. "If someone wanted to write for *Parenting Magazine*, it would probably help to state that he had kids."

The executive laughs, "Well you've definitely learned a lot."

The young man says, "I obviously have some changes to make to my resume thanks to the Third Key. We went over a lot. Is it alright if I review my notes with you?"

The executive says, "Sure, that's a good idea, then we'll go over polishing the keys."

The young man shows his mentor the bullet-pointed notes.

THE THIRD KEY
Resume Supporting Evidence

Education
- Not as important as experience.
- Often not important at all unless you attended one of the top institutions for your industry, especially in the creative arts.

Personal Information
- Only list information about your family, hobbies, or sport activities if it is relevant to the job and/or it will leave a positive impression.
- Statements that should be true for anyone (such as "I'm a people person") are often thought of as not being true or insincere.

Multi-lingual
- Always list your ability to speak or read a foreign language if you are fluent.

Software
- Don't include version numbers.

Awards
- Include only those relevant to your career.
- Acts as supporting evidence of your abilities.

Order of Information
- List the most relevant information to the employer first. This only works if you don't include dates.

This Resume Sucks
Software Version Numbers

Software Knowledge:
* Microsoft Word, Ver. 6.1
* Microsoft Photoshop, Version 6.0
* CorelDraw, Version 10
* Adobe Acrobat 5.0
* Windows NT/XP/ME
* Microsoft Excel 2000
* Powerpoint 2000

Education:
Associates In Science Degree
University of the South
Majors in Political Science & Software Development

Figure 11. Before

Each software listed specifies a version which makes your resume look outdated each time a new version is released. You could continually update your resume, assuming you stay current with every software change, but the resumes you already sent out would still make it appear to employers that you may not be familiar with the latest software version.

This Resume Rocks
Software Version Numbers

Software Knowledge:
* Word
* Photoshop
* CorelDraw
* Adobe Acrobat
* Excel
* Powerpoint

Education:
Associates In Science Degree
University of the South
Majors in Political Science & Software Development

Figure 12. After

With the software version numbers removed, your resume and your skill set always look up-to-date. Employers seldom ask which version you are familiar with and will assume the best.

Windows was also removed from the list since it's an operating system and not an application software. Listing it looks like you are padding your resume.

As an added note about software, always make sure that the names of the software are spelled correctly or it may look like you either aren't familiar with it or that you're careless. For instance, in Figure 12 CorelDraw should be changed to CorelDRAW and Powerpoint should be corrected to read PowerPoint.

This Resume Sucks
Education, Hobbies and Personal Information

MECHANICAL ENGINEER
John Public
407-555-1234

EDUCATION & TRAINING:
Master of Science, Mechanical Engineering - Carnegie-Mellon University, Pittsburgh, PA, 2001
Bachelor of Science - Monmouth University - Long Branch, NJ, 1974

HOBBIES:
Refurbishing motor boats
Tennis
Black Belt in Tae Kwon Do

PERSONAL:
Married for 35 years to Phyllis, a law-enforment officer
Three children, Luke and Reece (15) and Jean (21)
Chairman - Small Business Association Leads Group

Figure 13. Before

Many people place education at the top of their resumes, while most companies hire based on experience, not education. Education may be a factor, but it's a distant second or third to experience. Therefore, education should always be listed further down on a resume.

That said, Mr. Public has an engineering degree from Carnegie Mellon which is one of the most highly regarded schools in engineering. Any time you have a degree from one of the top schools in your field, it carries added significance. If your potential boss is from the same school (this takes some good research to find out,) it becomes even more important.

Mr. Public's graduation date and length of marriage tells us he's most likely in his 50's or 60's. Ageism is possible as some employers want younger employees. Some employers feel older employees will cost more, are slowing down in their career, or feel that older employees won't be as current as younger ones.

Removing dates eliminates these potential obstacles.

Mr. Public's hobbies don't necessarily support his resume. Refurbishing boats may be beneficial to include if he uses his engineering training for his hobby. It would be especially helpful to list his hobby if the company he was soliciting had anything to do with motors, boats or other vehicles. Including tennis on his resume is unlikely to support his career goals and should be omitted. His status as a black belt could be helpful, much the same way experience in the armed forces could be. Both martial arts and the armed forces teach discipline and focus. Having a black belt may also counter any ageism as it shows he is energetic and most likely fit.

The listed personal information has no place here, except for the Small Business Association credit. Marital status and being a parent are irrelevant to a job search unless it's for a position that deals with marriage or kids.

This Resume Rocks
Education, Hobbies and Personal Information

EDUCATION & TRAINING:
Master of Science, Mechanical Engineering - Carnegie-Mellon University
Bachelor of Science - Monmouth University

HOBBIES:
Refurbishing motor boats and motors
Black Belt in Tae Kwon Do

AFFILIATIONS:
Chairman - Small Business Association Leads Group

Figure 14. After

We removed all of the dates, which should take care of any discrimination based on age.

We also deleted the locations of the universities, since it doesn't matter and others typically know the location of the prestigious schools in their field.

Assuming that this resume is going to a company which has something to do with motors, boats or vehicles, we left in his refurbishing hobby. Otherwise we would have deleted it.

The black belt listing is impressive so we left that as well. Lower belts do not hold the same cachet, so we would not recommend listing yellow, blue, or brown belts.

Tennis has also been deleted. If Mr. Public was applying for a job at a tennis pro-shop or as a manager at a tennis racket manufacturing facility, then it would be very important to keep on his resume.

The Personal section was changed to Affiliations because we got rid of all his home life references. Employers are not looking for someone with a long marriage; they are looking for someone with impressive credits and credentials.

POLISHING YOUR KEYS
Resume Editing and Design

The executive says, "Well it looks like you've got the Third Key covered. Now let's talk about polishing the keys. Polishing is when you check for any mistakes and layout problems and make sure your resume shines. A polished key helps create a great first impression."

The young man adds, "And I've learned what NOT to put."

The executive continues, "Exactly. Putting the wrong sorts of information on your resume could create an unfavorable or incorrect image. Something else that creates an image of you is the overall appearance of your resume. Your resume should convey that you are meticulous, organized, focused, and professional."

The young man looks at his resume, "Does my resume say that about me?"

The executive takes the young man's resume, "Let's look at the resume you faxed to me as if we were recruiters. I want you to examine it with an eye for presentation only. Your faxed resume is much darker than it should be because you used colored paper and the faxed graphics are now ugly, unrecognizable splotches*[16]. Plus this font in particular is unreadable. It would have been a problem if you had e-mailed it to me as well. I don't believe I have this font on my computer, so who knows what it would have looked like? Use standard typefaces such as Times New Roman, New Century Schoolbook, Courier and Palatino or sans-serif fonts such as Helvetica, Arial, Futura, Geneva, and Univers. Plus a font size of 10 to 12 points is best and avoid fancy font styles such as shadows, underline, italics and those with extremely thin lines. Boldface and capital letters are acceptable to use especially to differentiate headers from the rest of the text as long as the letters don't touch each other."

The young man asks, "It seems like it might be a good idea to have a version of my resume that's just for scanning and one that I use for more traditional presentation?"

The executive enthusiastically agrees, "You could do that, but you may not know if a resume you send to someone will be scanned or not. Here are a few more tips about scannable resumes." The executive pulls a piece of paper out of one of his desk drawers that he hands to the young man. It's labeled Scannable Resumes.

The young man glances at it and says, "This is awesome!"

Scannable Resumes

A scannable resume has the same information as a traditional resume – it's the formatting that may make it different. Using keywords, proper format, and font/typestyle are important because computer software is highly sensitive and a database search is generally conducted with nouns and keywords most often used by that particular employer's industry.

Format

- Left justify the entire document
- Place your name and job title at the top of the page on their own lines
- Use white or light-colored 8 x 11 paper.
- Provide a laser-printed original, if possible.
- Do not fold or staple.
- Avoid vertical and horizontal lines, graphics, and boxes.
- Use standard address format below your name.
- If you have more than one address, one should be placed on top of the other.

Joe East
22 Black Creek Lane
Kansas City, KS 88888

Joe East
2555 Long Street
Kansas City, KS 88888

- List each phone number on its own line.
- Use only those abbreviations that are familiar in your field.
- Use more nouns than action verbs. For example, using a noun, such as, "set designer" is preferable to "designer of sets."

Keywords

Keywords are the most important part of your scannable resume. You can either incorporate them into your experience section or you can include a keyword summary at the end of your resume.

Keywords are words that are commonly used in a particular industry. For example, an animator might use words like "creating," "design," and "character building" in the experience section. But don't forget to turn those words into useful nouns like "key animator," and "digital illustrator."

Several experts suggest using a keyword summary at the end of the scannable resume.* Here's an example:

Systems engineering Bachelor of Science degree Experience with power engineering consulting firm and municipal utility Research in human machine interface of maintenance subsystem designs and procedures Staff budget and inventory manager for small business

Font / Typestyle

- Use standard type faces such as Times New Roman, New Century, Schoolbook, Courier, and Palatino or sans-serif fonts such as Helvetica, Arial, Futura, Geneva, and Univers.

- Use a font size of 10 to 12 points.

- Avoid fancy font styles such as *italics,* underline, and shadows.

- **Boldface** and CAPITAL letters are acceptable as long as the letters don't touch   each other.

- Provide white space between words.

  For example: separate an area code from its phone number with a space rather than parentheses: 765 123 - 4567 (also notice the space before and after the hyphen).

- Avoid condensing the space between letters because they may touch.

- Avoid using special characters such as bullets.

Mailing Tips

- Do not fold or staple the scannable resume.

- Mail in a 9 1/2 x 12 envelopes.

If you are concerned about the status of your application (unless explicitly stated otherwise) call your contact or the human resources department of your potential employer.

The young man says, "So I should put my resume on white paper with no graphics? That seems boring."

The executive counters, "Let me put it this way. If you had been applying for a job here and I got this faxed resume from you it would end up..." He turns on his paper shredder and puts the young man's resume through the shredder. "...here."

The young man says, "That's cold."

The executive says, "That's the cold reality. This company receives hundreds of resumes a week and if you think any of us have time to decipher what your garbled fax says, or reformat your e-mailed resume, you're mistaken. Speaking of which, how do you have the file of your resume saved?"

The young man responds, "I have it saved as a Word document named resume.doc. Why?"

The executive replies, "With the high volume of resumes we get every day, a file simply named resume.doc is sure to get lost in the system since most people misname their files like you did. You should title your file with your name, such as johnsmithresume.doc. Or better yet, include the job title and call your file John_Smith_Salesman_Resume.doc. This will help us find and track your resume.*[17]"

The young man says, "Okay. That makes sense. So I should use common fonts for e-mail files and have a plain resume on white paper that I fax and another version that I hand out or mail."

The executive says, "You could do that, but I suggest that you only print your resume on plain, white paper. That way, you're certain that it will fax well, be readable under any circumstances, and look professional. I may want to fax the resume you hand me to an associate at another company. Always run a test fax, and then fax the faxed resume again. Many times people pass along resumes by copy or fax so it's quite possible that your resume could get faxed or copied twice*[18]. You should also test your original resume and a faxed version to see if it can be scanned into a database. Some HR departments will not file resumes that can't be scanned to OCR (Optical Character Recognition*[19]), where your resume will be used in search programs. Many large companies keep digitized versions of resumes on file to limit space and enhance usability*[20]. If you keep the presentation simple and professional you shouldn't have a problem. Let the information, not the graphic in the corner, capture the readers' attention."

"OK. But, what about if someone wanted to include his picture on his resume?" The young man asked.

"He should never do it," says the boss. "You never know if your looks, age, or race could be a negative in the eyes of the beholder. So don't take any chances."

The executive continues, "Now let's search for spelling errors, punctuation, and grammar mistakes and anything else that might be distracting."

The young man says, "Alright. I did use spell check though, so I doubt we'll find any spelling mistakes."

The executive says, "Let's start at the top. You've crossed out your phone number and hand-written another number under it."

The young man explains, "That's because I just moved two days ago and my computer was in boxes and I couldn't change it."

The executive says, "I don't care if your dog ate your computer. The best excuse in the world does not merit crossing things out on a resume and having any sort of hand-written information. It looks sloppy and it says that you're lazy because you didn't take the small amount of time required to change it properly on the computer. There are always stores that have computers to rent and friends with computers to borrow. Try keeping a disk of your resume on hand or post it on the internet so you always have access to it*[21]."

The young man nods a little sheepishly.

"I mentioned the graphics you have on your resume a

few moments ago," continues the executive. "Illustrations of any sort are not a good idea on a resume."

"What about designers and artists? Wouldn't they need to have art and designs on their resumes?" counters the young man.

"That's what portfolios are for," responds the executive. "Remember how bad your graphics looked when they came over on a fax? And you never know if someone will fax one of your resumes to someone else. Plus, since many of us scan resumes now, the graphics won't translate. In fact, even fancy fonts could make the scan of your resume useless*[22]. Scanning is also why you should only print your resume on one side of the paper."

Make your resume e-friendly.

"I guess that's why colored paper is also a problem," says the young man.

"I see you also typed your name in all lower case letters," says the executive.

The young man responds, "I like the way names in all lower case look on posters I've seen."

The boss counters, "It makes you look meek. Plus it's just incorrect and registers that way in the mind of the reader."

"Before you do your final check, you need to make sure you've included your key words," says the executive.

"You mean like great and efficient. Words that make me sound better?" says the young man.

"No," states the executive. "Words like manager, writer, BA, Spanish, software terms, and industry acronyms should be included. Job listings will help determine some of the words you should include. When companies scan resumes, they often search through them using key words relevant to any open positions*[23]."

The executive continues, "You mentioned you used spell check which is always a good idea, but you can't rely on it to catch everything. Here's a great example of why not. You meant to use the word waste in this job description, but instead you typed waist. Both are spelled correctly so the software wouldn't have highlighted it. I actually received a resume recently with a fatal typo; the intended job title was Shift Manager, but the applicant left the "f" out…and he didn't work for the sanitation department."

"Asking others," continues the boss, "to proofread your resume is always a good idea. You can also print out your document and read each word out loud while you point to each word with your finger*[24]. As you do this, don't pay attention to content. Focus only on the words and punctuation. You should always review for content before this final proofreading step."

The boss hands the young man his resume and says, "Here. You try it."

The young man reads his resume out loud as he points to each word. He gets down to the Second Key where his job experience is listed and he stops. "Hey, look. I just noticed something. In the first two jobs I listed, I put the job titles in bold and in the last two I didn't."

The boss beams, "See that was a good catch. A formatting mistake like that seems minor, but I know that I'm a stickler for details and when I notice inconsistencies, I'm distracted and I assume that the person is not very careful. Well keep going. See what else you can find."

The young man finishes proofreading his resume. He says, "I didn't find anything else wrong."

The executive says, "Good. I didn't either. Now let's check your resume for aesthetics. In other words, make it pleasing to the eye." They both look at it and the boss continues, "I suggest you separate areas of information with a blank line. For example, your job experience blends into the Third Key.

Also, your e-mail address is too small. If this were a fax or if I made a poor copy of it, your e-mail would be unreadable."

"Another thing I noticed," he continues, "is that you write full sentences as descriptions for your additional jobs responsibilities."

"Yes," the young man says proudly. "Ms. Finley said I should only describe duties that went beyond my actual job title."

"True," says the executive. "But you have to be mindful of the short amount of time I will spend looking at your resume. Don't make me read it. I should be able to scan it and see all of the important information. Otherwise, I may miss something."

The young man says, "That makes sense. I guess I could have a few short bullet points under each job title."

"Exactly," says the boss. "With those elements corrected, it will look good. Well...that wraps up our session for today unless you have any more questions."

The young man says, "I do have a question about using humor as part of my resume. I have a friend who puts on his resume References Upon Subpoena and titles his job experience with Experiences That I Admit To. He told me that one time he got a call from someone he had sent his resume to because the guy said that anyone who was so flippant on his resume must be good enough to back it up. What's your opinion of using humor?"

The executive answers, "Well it depends on the type of career you have. Typically those involved in creative work appreciate a unique and perhaps humorous approach. Lawyers and bankers on the other hand usually prefer resumes with no frills. You should research and know your audience. If there's any chance that trying to be funny could put someone off, then don't do it. The other part of the equation is you. If you're not the kind of person who's comfortable cracking jokes in an interview, then don't be funny on your resume. Otherwise it's kind of like false advertising. Remember your resume represents *who* you are. So did your friend get an interview based on his resume?"

The young man replies, "Yes, but not a job with that company. The manager didn't have anything at that time, but he did pass my friend's resume on to a colleague of his who did eventually hire my friend."

The executive says, "Well you have some good stories of your own."

The young man gets up and gathers his things to leave. He says, "Thank you for all of your help. I've learned so much that it's a little overwhelming. I know I need to polish my three keys and then I will send my resume to you."

The executive says, "Great. I look forward to receiving it."

As the young man exits the office, he smiles to himself knowing that the 3 Keys to a Successful Resume WILL open the doors to the perfect job.

POLISHING THE THREE KEYS
Resume Editing and Design

Format & Design

- Layout should make it easy to read at a glance.
- Bullet points read faster than sentences.
- Bolding, indents and bullets should be consistent throughout.
- Text should be 10 point or larger and clear enough to read if faxed twice.
- Never include graphics or photos. They don't fax or scan well.
- Your name and title should always be capitalized.
- Never hand-correct a resume.
- Use plain white paper so it will scan and fax properly.

Proofread

- Print out your resume and say each word out loud as you touch it with your finger. Have others proofread your resume.
- Misspellings, grammar and punctuation errors are unprofessional and careless. You don't want your resume to look like shift.

Fonts

- Fancy fonts often don't scan properly into databases.
- Uncommon fonts may not be available to recipients when e-mailed.

- Use standard type faces such as Times New Roman, New Century
  Schoolbook, Courier, and Palatino or sans-serif fonts such as Helvetica, Arial, Futura, Geneva, and Univers.

Customization

- Customize resumes for each employer and each position.
- Use industry key words and key words from job listings and company literature to enhance your resumes results in a database search.

Humor

- Use only if the industry and employer make use of it.
- Use only if you are naturally funny.

Bullet points read faster than sentences.

This Resume Sucks
Hand-Written Edits

Figure 15. Before

Job seekers often print many copies of their resume and then make hand-written corrections when some of their information changes.

In this example, John Public is communicating a lack of respect for himself and shows recruiters they were not worth the extra effort to re-type the information.

This Resume Rocks
Hand-Written Edits

Salesperson
John Public
407-555-6789 home
407-555-9876 mobile

Experience:
Shoes-2-Tight - Orlando, Fl
    Salesman of the Month four times in one year.

Clothing X-Pensive - Dallas, TX
    * Sales
    * Display design

Figure 16. After

Notice how much more professional the resume looks when everything is typed.

With computers, there is never an excuse for not having an up-to-date resume. If you are relocating make sure you have a digital copy of your resume so you can revise it even when your computer is still packed. You can borrow a computer or rent one at a location such as Kinko's.

An easy and inexpensive way to have your resume always available for editing is to e-mail a copy of your resume to your e-mail account and leave it on the server. You can set up a free e-mail account at www.yahoo.com or www.msn.com and store files which can be accessed from anywhere in the world at any time.

When you put your home and mobile numbers on your resume, make sure the messages on your answering services are appropriately professional.

This Resume Sucks
Graphics and Photos

DESIGN-R-US
Logo design, t-shirt design, print ads

CLOTHING X-PENSIVE
Air brushed t-shirts

Figure 17. Before

DESIGN-R-US
Logo design, t-shirt design, print ads

CLOTHING X-PENSIVE
Air brushed t-shirts

Figure 18. Scanned page

This Resume Sucks
Graphics and Photos

Many designers think they should load up their resumes with graphics and beautiful illustrations. The place to show off art is in portfolios.

Notice how awful the graphics and photos look after being scanned or copied. OCR scans would kick this resume out. Even if this resume were e-mailed, many systems would not accept the images. Your photo should never be on your resume anyway.

The fonts lose both their appeal and readability when poorly scanned and copied. The shadowed text experience becomes almost unreadable. The phone number can barely be read as well.

This Resume Rocks
Graphics & Photos

GRAPHIC DESIGNER
John Public
407-555-1234

Experience:
Design-R-Us
　　　Logo design, t-shirt design, print ads

Clothing X-Pensive
　　　Air brushed t-shirts

Figure 19. After

While this version may not have great graphic design, it serves its purpose with a clean and easy-to-read presentation that accurately delivers its message. It will fax, copy, and scan cleanly.

Designers and artists have portfolios that showcase their abilities; while, the purpose of the resume is to list experience.

Including visuals on a resume looks amateurish because professionals know better.

This Resume Sucks
Fonts and OCR

DADirect, Inc.
Accounting Manager
Responsible for general bookkeeping activities and practices in the office and to participate in reviewing and appraising financial procedures and records. Making General Journal entries and posting to the General Ledger.
Preparing monthly balance sheet and income statement using Peachtree Accounting software. Preparing Excel reports with sales, cost of sales and gross/net profit margin analysis. Cash management plus responsible for accounts payable and accounts receivable. Analysis of financial statement and perform month-end financial closing and and process bank and general ledger reconciliation. Answers all vendor inquiries with professionalism and accuracy. Additional responsibilities may include auditing expense reports, supplier/vendor set up and check processing.

LBI, DALLAS, TEXAS
ACCOUNTING MANAGER
Responsible for supervising accounting department, prepare monthly financial package, prepare year end audit package, reconcile general ledger. Also prepares annual budgets, maintain company's accounting systems, and many other duties. This person reports directly to the President of the company, Mr. Murphy.

Figure 20. Before OCR

Above is a section of a resume with many different fonts to illustrate the options you have in designing the look of your resume.

Plain serif and non-serif fonts are best for resumes. They are easiest to read and are properly recognized during optical character recognition (OCR). OCR is performed when a document is faxed or mailed to a company and then is digitized (scanned) into a database.

The following page shows the results of OCR on this resume.

This Resume Rocks
Fonts and OCR

DADirect, Inc.
Acceuntins 8mgasr
@on&& f n-7 Lvt/-aL him &m/x/n3 mzlwtt*m and/la&lcrn m hc&f~t/ cvrndti~/~~w/kacto MZ. P C ~ Z Y O M Z . ~
cvmd ~ & $ l ~ f f / d ~ f l ~ f M Z . {C ~ / ~ O ~ C & P & ff/jid7~7& Ju~/:3 g f f f &/& amdbf~hfi3 fn- g e / z . C ~
f f L -tdl
Preparing monthly balance sheet and income statement using Peachtree Accounting sofiare. Przparing Excel
reports with sales, cost of sales andgoss/net profit mg@ analysis. Cash management plus responsible fir accounts
payable and accounts receivable. Analysis offinancial statement and perfirm month-end financial closing and
process bank andgeneral ledger reconciliation. Answers all vendor inquiries with prof2:ssionalism and accuracy.
Additional responsibilities may include auditing expense reports, supplier/venddo set up and check processing.

LBI, DALLAS, TEXAS
aec@@m4MS 4bm'dUG&@
RasponsiTinie for snnpervisimg aooannnfing dapartmamt, prepaira montTinly 1Finamoiall paolinage, prepare yam
amd adit racomcile gameran L&en

Also prepares annual budgets, maintain company's accounting systems,
and many other duties. This person reports directly to the President of the company, Mr. Murphy.

Figure 21. After OCR

The top line and the bottom two sentences are the same font and the only plain non-serif fonts in the document. They are also the only ones that converted perfectly into editable text during OCR.

The rest of the text is a mess. We've underlined all the text that was converted incorrectly. You will notice the top Accounting Manager title and the fancy cursive text under it did not translate at all.

The second paragraph of text converted better, but still had 12 mistakes which translates to an almost 17% failure rate.

Avoid using decorative fonts (Script, Calligrapher, etc.) and stick with the more simple Serif Fonts (Times Roman, Bookman, etc.), or the very simple Sans Serif Fonts (Arial, Tahoma, Helvetica, etc.)

The fine line font near the bottom had an 88% OCR failure rate.

This Resume Sucks
Typos and Bullets

Nissan Motor Acceptance Corporation (01/97-present)

Senior Customer Account Representative
(promoted from Lease Custmer Service Representative)

Being fluent in PowerPoint, I have been able to provide reports that get the **true** picture of the material requested. My communication and written skills contributes to the " **1 call does it all**" approach dramatically improving customer satisfaction. My extensive product knowledge has contributed to the successful **coaching, ongoing training,** and **development** of the CSR's. As a result of this knowledge and communication skills, I have been assigned to lead Corporate tours and introduce and familiarize visitors with the activities and importance of our department. I consistently initiate and implement **motivational ideas** within the department, causing our agents to exceed standards, resulting in a **Leadership award** presented by the Department Director and Manager.

Allied Marketing Group, INC. (08/87-06/95)
Shit Manager

  * Promoted from Shift Manger to CS Supervisor to Asst. CS Manager

I was given the opportunity in a *Management* position to utilize my **problem solving** skills in **redesigning** the Customer Service Department to accommodate more people and provide better service. I was able to conduct ninety-day and annual reviews providing **important feed back** to the representatives and and giving them the tools and coaching needed to fulfill their departmental goals. **Accuracy and detail** contributed to the successfully design, layout, and editing of all brochures and literature. I was completely **responsible** for insuring that the products, verbiage, and placement of all brochures and literature were accurate and effective before submitting to final production.

Figure 22. Before

The information on this resume is so dense that it's hard to glance through it and get an overall idea of this person's experience.

Bold and italics are also used incorrectly. Keywords have been bolded which is unnecessary, a distraction and incorrect formatting. Management in the first line of the second paragraph is in italics which is incorrect formatting as well.

Notice the title Shit Manager. This is doubtfully how she feels about the quality of her work, but rather a very unfortunate typo. After an employer finished laughing, she would probably throw this resume away because carelessness on a resume would most likely mean carelessness at the work place.

Formatting is also inconsistent. The lines under their job titles are handled differently in both cases. One is in parenthesis and the other is tabbed with a bullet. The bottom paragraph is also indented, while the top one is not.

The word and is repeated in the bottom paragraph (at the end of one line and at the beginning of the following line.) Manager is also misspelled in the job description just under Shit Manager.

There is at least one more misspelling. Can you find it?

This Resume Rocks
Typos and Bullets

Nissan Motor Acceptance Corporation
Senior Customer Account Representative
* Built PowerPoint reports.
* Coached, trained and developed CSR's.
* Lead corporate tours.
* Recipient of Leadership Award.
* Initiate and implement motivational ideas.

Allied Marketing Group, INC.
Shift Manager
* Redesigned Customer Service Department for more people and better service.
* Conducted a 90 day and annual reviews.
* Designed, and edited all brochures and literature.

Figure 23. After

We removed all the bold, italics and capitalizations that didn't make sense. We also lost the dates and the promotion lines. Her promotions were not as important as where she ended up.

We added the "f" back into Shift and made the entire layout consistent.

The biggest overall change we made was to re-format all the verifiable elements (non-subjective) from full sentences to bullet-pointed information. Because the resume is cleaner and more clear, it's more likely to get read.

SUMMARY OF THE
THREE KEYS TO SUCCESS

THE FIRST KEY
Resume Header

Job Title
- Clearly state the job title for which you are applying and if possible include a job code or job requisition number.
- The job title is more important than your name.
- Find out what jobs are available and customize your resume to the job that you are interested in and that your work history supports.

Objective Statement
- Do not include an objective statement.
- Include a branding statement which is a more powerful sales tool. State something positive and verifiable.
- Or if you have glowing remarks that someone made about your job performance in writing, you can put that on your resume.

Contact Information
- Make it large enough, 10 to 12 point, so even a bad fax machine won't make it unreadable.
- Don't use your current employer's phone number or your e-mail at work. Employers often track their employees' e-mail.

THE SECOND KEY
Resume Experience

Dates
- Do not list dates because they can give away your age and lead to incorrect and negative conclusions.

Job Departure
- Never list reasons for leaving a job because they always leave negative impressions and read like excuses.

Experience
- Include all relevant experiences - paid and unpaid.
- List the most relevant experience first, not the most recent.

Be Truthful
- Lying on a resume will catch up to you and could cost you your job.

List Results
- Employers hire others who produce results. Instead of obvious job descriptions, list concrete and verifiable results.

The Job Duh Factor
- Don't list duties which are obvious from each job title.

Extra Job Duties
- Highlight your duties above and beyond your job title.

THE THIRD KEY
Resume Supporting Evidence

Education
- Not as important as experience, unless you attended one of the top institutions for your industry.
- Not always necessary to list especially in creative industries.

Personal Information
- Only list information about your family, hobbies, or sport activities if it is relevant to the job and it will leave a positive impression.
- Statements that should be true for anyone (such as, "I'm a people person.") are often thought of as not being true or insincere.

Multi-lingual
- Always list your ability to speak or read a foreign language if you are fluent.

Software
- Don't include version numbers.

Awards
- Include only those relevant to your career.
- Acts as supporting evidence of your abilities.

Order of Information
- List the most relevant information to the employer first. This only works if you don't include dates.

POLISHING THE THREE KEYS
Resume Editing and Design

Format & Design
- Layout should make it easy to read at a glance.
- Bullet points read faster than sentences.
- Bold, indents and bullets should be consistent throughout.
- Text should be large and clear enough to read if faxed twice.
- Never include graphics or photos. They don't fax or scan well.
- Your name and title should always be capitalized.
- Never hand-correct a resume.
- Use plain white paper so it will scan and fax properly.

Proofread
- Print out your resume and say each word out loud as you touch it with your finger. Have others proofread your resume.
- Misspellings, grammar and punctuation errors are unprofessional and careless. You don't want your resume to look like shift.

Fonts

- Fancy fonts often don't scan into databases.
- Uncommon fonts may not be available to recipient when e-mailed.
- Use standard type faces such as Times New Roman, New Century Schoolbook, Courier, and Palatino or sans-serif fonts such as Helvetica, Arial, Futura, Geneva, and Univers.

Customization

- Customize resumes for each employer and each position.
- Use industry key words and key words from job listings and company literature to enhance your resumes results in a database search.

Humor

- Use only if the industry and employer make use of it.
- Use only if you are naturally funny.

Before and After Resume Examples

In this section you'll find resumes that were actually sent to us. Names and addresses have been changed to protect the job seekers. For each resume, we point out what needs to be changed, followed by a revised rockin' resume and an explanation of what we changed and why.

There's nothing like actual examples to get points across, so study each one carefully and see how your resume compares.

This Resume Sucks

Johnny Anonymous
555-555-1234
who@somewebsite.com
111 Some Drive
Somewhere, TX 77777

OBJECTIVE: A challenging position within Nissan, which can provide an opportunity for me to apply my broad capabilities and business experience.

SUMMARY OF QUALIFICATIONS

- 11 years of diverse work experience
- Quick study, comfortable with the challenge of new methods and applications

EDUCATION AND TRAINING

University of North Texas   Master's of Science   2004 – Present
Denton, Texas   Real Estate Analysis

University of North Texas Bachelor of Business Administration   2002
Denton, Texas   Finance Major
- Electives were Corporation Law, Cost Accounting, Financial Statement Analysis, Risk Management, Real Estate Investments, and Real Estate Management
- Member of the Real Estate Club

Tarrant County College Associate in Arts   1998 – 2000
Hurst, Texas

Sky Helicopters   Commercial Helicopter License   1997 – 1998
Garland, Texas

EMPLOYMENT HISTORY

NMAC   Credit Analyst   2004 – Present

Irving, Texas
- Review car loan applications presented by Nissan dealerships for acceptance by NMAC.

NMAC   Lease Customer Network   2002 – 2004

Irving, Texas
- Advise lease customers about the end-of-lease procedures, resolve and correct liability issues, and provide support to customer service.

Sieben Management   Office Manager   1998 – Present
N. Richland Hills, Texas Self-employed
- Execute the administrative and financial operations of an optometry office; negotiate office and equipment leases, legal and tax issues, insurance and staffing requirements.

Merrill Lynch   Research Assistant   2001
Plano, Texas   Internship
- Researched publicly traded companies and financial market conditions; prepared and analyzed special projects and studies as assigned by advisors.

This Resume Sucks

Content
No Job Title – He clearly has experience, but we have no idea what job he's seeking.

Objective statement – This one is a good example of the person who is applying for the job stating what he wants to gain, not what he can contribute to the company. Consequently, it leaves a negative impression and is definitely a waste of time to read.

Summary of Qualifications - Not bad, but it would be much more effective if it supported a specific job title.

Order - Putting education before work experience makes it seem as though he has minimal experience which is not the case. Education, with rare exceptions, should go at the end of the resume along with any relevant hobbies or other personal information.

Dates – The inclusion of dates is confusing since he has two entries that have a beginning year and an end date as Present. Is he holding two jobs at once?

Personal information – Chances are that the fact that he has his commercial helicopter license is not pertinent to the job and should be deleted.

Internships – They count as much as any other work and shouldn't necessarily be listed last under work experience. Many internships are paid positions and doing an internship shows your initiative.

Design, Formatting, Proofreading

Job Titles - In the work experience section he lists Lease Customer Network as a job title and it is not. He couldn't have been a network, but he could have been an associate or manager.

Spacing – The indents on the information throughout the resume are inconsistent and should be avoided because such formatting does not hold up when e-mailed.

Verb Tense – When referring to past work all verb tenses should be consistently past.

This Resume Rocks

Credit Manager
Johnny Anonymous
555-555-1234
who@somewebsite.com

EMPLOYMENT HISTORY

Credit Analyst
NMAC
- Reviewed car loan applications

Lease Customer Network Associate
NMAC
- Advised lease customers about the end-of-lease procedures
- Resolved and corrected liability issues

Office Manager
Sieben Management
- Negotiated office and equipment leases
- Handled legal and tax issues
- Oversaw staffing requirements

Research Assistant - Internship
Merrill Lynch
- Researched publicly traded companies and financial market conditions
- Prepared and analyzed special projects

EDUCATION AND TRAINING

University of North Texas
Master of Science
Real Estate Analysis

University of North Texas
Bachelor of Business Administration
Finance Major
- Corporation Law
- Cost Accounting
- Financial Statement Analysis

This Resume Rocks

Content
Job Title - We created a job title from his most recent experience and advanced his career goal from analyst to manager.

Order - His work history is now listed first instead of his education.

Dates - All dates have been removed.

Job Locations – All locations of jobs have been removed since it should have little relevance as to where he can work.

Education - We removed the information about his county college schooling since is did not support his job title.

Design, Formatting, Proofreading
Point size – On a full–size sheet of paper, we made the point size larger for the entire resume from 10 to 12 point. The actual point size in the example for the book is 10 point. With the contact information larger, it will be readable no matter how it's transmitted. Never have any type smaller than 10 point and always make it larger if you can. In this case, the larger point size also filled out the paper without spilling over onto a second page.

Bullet Points – We replaced the full sentences with bullet-pointed information which makes it easier to absorb quickly and creates more inviting white space.

This Resume Sucks

JEANNE PAPPAS SIMON
PRODUCER

PRODUCER

Suburban Cinderella   A&S Animation, Inc.
Animated series short

International Blues Clues   Nickelodeon Network
Pilot for UK and Latin America

The Winkles: Material Girl - Animated Pilot   A&S Animation, Inc.
Creator, producer, writer
* Winner of two international film festival awards

Network Development   Turner Broadcasting
                                             Scott Sassa - Pres.
                                             Turner Entertainment
                                             Group

Series Development   Animal Planet

Carrot Top's A.M. Mayhem   Cartoon Network
Cartoon Networks first live-action series

Weinerville   Nickelodeon Network
Season 2
* Nominated for Ace Award 1994   *Kevin Kay - Exec. in*
Best short form program   *Charge of Production*

Commercials, industrials, documentaries   West End Prods

407-351-0893   *Jeanne@YourResumeSucks.biz*

LINE PRODUCER/ ASSOCIATE PRODUCER/SEGMENT PRODUCER

Roller Jam
Segment producer, writer, director

The Nashville Network
Brian Gadinsky-
Producer

Zoo Venture
Segment producer & director

Animal Planet

Allegra's Window

Nickelodeon Network
Jim Jenkins - Exec.
Prod.

Gullah Gullah Island

Nickelodeon Network
Kathy Minton
Maria Perez
Executive Producers
Kit Laybourne - Cr. Dir.

Clarissa Explains It All
Seasons 2-5
* Nominated for Emmy 1994

* Nominated for Ace Award 1993

Nickelodeon Network

Mitchell Kriegman -
Executive Producer
Chris Gifford-
Producer

Roundhouse

Nickelodeon Network

UNIT MANAGER

Clarissa Explains It All

Nickelodeon Network
*Mitchell Kriegman -
Executive Producer*

Real Mature

ABC/Nickelodeon,
Roger Price - Producer

What Would You Do?

Nickelodeon Network
*Woody Frasier - Prod
Bonnie Karrin - Prod*

Nick Arcade

Nickelodeon Network

Get The Picture

Nickelodeon Network
Marjorie Cohn - Prod

Make the Grade

Nickelodeon Network
*Angie Bartenbach -
Prod.*

PRODUCTION COORDINATOR

Lethal Weapon II
Feature film special unit

Warner Brothers
 *Michael Thau-
Director/Producer
Richard Donner-
Producer*

HBO Fall 1989 Previews

HBO, TV promos
*Elizabeth Hummer –
Prod.*

Perfume of the Cyclone

Toron Screen Corp.
Marlon Staggs - Prod

1st and Ten

HBO, TV series
Art Dept. Coordinator
*Jonathan Debin -
Dawn Tarnofsky - Prod*

Exec.

*407-351-0893
Jeanne@YourResumeSucks.biz*

Nowhere To Run   American Independent Pictures
                                            Julie Corman – Prod.

Numerous Commercials   Bill Moffitt and
                                            Assoc.
                                            Bill Moffitt - Exec.
Prod.

OTHER STUFF
Writer:
Secrets of the Animal Kingdom (2 scripts)   Walt Disney TV
Weekly syndicated series for ages 4-12

Winkles: Material Girl   A&S, Inc.
6 min. Animated pilot for preschoolers.
Winner of 2 International awards

Timmy's Lessons in Nature   A&S, Inc.
Development

Suburban Cinderella   A&S, Inc.
Animated presentation. Winner of 5 international awards

Nickelodeon production management guide book

Created production guide book for Nickelodeon based on *International Blues Clues* test

Written and developed numerous TV show pitch packages

407-351-0893
Jeanne@YourResumeSucks.biz

This Resume Sucks

Overall

There is much too much information. Believe me (Jeanne), when I revised my resume it was hard to simplify it by eliminating credits. Nobody likes to do it because we know every project we've worked on has made us who we are today and we want to share with potential employers every single job. That's the biggest reason sometimes to hire someone to write your resume because she can be brutally objective and only include information that the employer would be interested in reviewing.

* Note: This resume on 8.5x11 paper is only two pages long. When we formatted this book it stretched to four pages.

I divided my resume into two separate resumes each targeting a different job: producer and writer. Having two resumes allows me to make the strongest case for myself when I apply for a position without confusing anyone.

Content

- Don't need writer credits on my producer resume. Being a writer is always something I can bring up in an interview or mention, if appropriate, in a cover letter.
- The credits under the Unit Manager and Production Coordinator headings should be abbreviated. It is not as important as what is on the first page.

Design, Formatting, Proofreading

Contact information – It's in the footer and not where most people would look for at it at the top of the resume. Making anyone work to find your phone number is a bad idea.

Job title – It should be at the top of the page instead of my name.

Order of work experience – Put most impressive credits first in any grouping. If someone just skims my resume, they will most likely read the first few credits under a heading most carefully and skim over the rest. Remember, you have about 3 seconds to make an impression – make it a great one!

Columns – This type of format tends not to hold when it's e-mailed and the information gets so jumbled that it's hard to make sense out of it.

This Resume Rocks

PRODUCER
JEANNE PAPPAS SIMON
(407)351-0893

Jeanne@YourResumeSucks.biz

"One of the most respected producers in children's television today."
- Mitchell Kriegman
Creator of Bear In the Big Blue House & Clarissa Explains It All

Work Experience
Producer
Nickelodeon Network
International Blues Clues
- Pilot for UK and Latin America
- Live-action with virtual sets

Weinerville
- Nominated for Ace Award - Best short form program
- Live-action interstitials with puppets

Turner Broadcasting
- Network Development
- Created content, budgets, schedules and staffing

Cartoon Network
- Carrot Top's A.M. Mayhem
  - Network's first live-action production

A&S Animation, Inc
Timmy's Lessons in Nature
- Animated shorts that won Grand Prize in Nicktoons Festival

The Winkles: Material Girl
- Animated Pilot
- Winner of two international film festival awards

1-2

Producer   (407) 351-0893

Jeanne Pappas Simon
Jeanne@YourResumeSucks.biz

Line Producer/Associate Producer/Segment Producer

The Nashville Network
Roller Jam
- Segment producer, writer, director
- Live-action "reality" show
- Brian Gadinsky - Producer

Nickelodeon Network
Allegra's Window
- Series with puppets
- Jim Jenkins - Executive Producer

Clarissa Explains It All
- Live-action series
- Mitchell Kriegman - Executive Producer
- Chris Gifford - Producer

Roundhouse
- Live-action skit comedy series
- Rita Sheffield - Executive Producer

Animal Planet
Zoo Venture
- Segment producer & director of live-action roll-ins

Unit Manager

Nickelodeon Network
- Clarissa Explains It All
- Real Mature
- What Would You Do?
- Nick Arcade

Production Coordinator

Clients include: Warner Brothers, HBO, American Independent Pictures
(Roger Corman's production company) , & numerous commercials

2-2

This Resume Rocks

Overall
Now my (Jeanne) resume presents a stronger image of me as a competent, experienced, and respected producer because it's better organized, only contains relevant information, and highlights a quote by Mitchell Kriegman who is one of the most prolific and respected creators of children's TV.

Content
Names – I only left in the names of those I worked with who I felt were well known in the industry.

Description - Since I deleted my writing credits, I had room to add a bit of description to some credits like Live-action skit comedy series or Series with puppets so a potential employer could see the variety and breadth of my experience.

Design, Formatting, Proofreading
Contact Information – All my contact information is easy to find at the top of pages 1 and 2. That way if they get separated, anyone will know to whom page 2 belongs. All contact information is in 12 point size or larger.

Font – Palatino is the font because it's easy to read and does well with OCR.

Job Title – On the first page it is bold and in 16 point size. Make the job title on your resume the size that looks the best with the overall design of your resume, but do make it bigger than your name.

Placement - Most of the information is left justified and bullet-pointed which makes it easy to scan and creates a resume with a lot of white space that's inviting to read. Plus this type of formatting should not move around too much when e-mailed.

This Resume Rocks

WRITER
JEANNE PAPPAS SIMON
(407)351-0893
Jeanne@YourResumeSucks.biz

Grand Prize Winner in Nicktoons Film Festival

Writer/Wordsmith
Walt Disney TV Productions/Hearst Entertainment
Secrets of the Animal Kingdom (2 scripts)

A&S Animation, Inc
Timmy's Lessons in Nature
- Grand Prize in Nicktoons Film Festival
- ASIFA East award for Excellence in Writing

Winkles: Material Girl   .
- 6 minute animated pilot for preschoolers
- Winner of 2 international awards

Suburban Cinderella
- Animated short
- Winner of 5 international awards

MEGA Entertainment
Bug Off/ Buzz Off
- Animated series pilot, development, bible

Written and developed numerous TV show pitch packages and bibles

Your Resume Sucks!
- A book about how to write an attention-grabbing resume using the 3 Keys to Success

Producer
Over 400 episodes of TV for Nickelodeon, Cartoon Network, TNN, etc

This Resume Rocks

Overall

My writer resume is not nearly as deep as my producer resume, but it does the job of showing off my credits and accomplishments. My producing credits support my writing abilities as it shows my production experience. I can always mention my specific producer credentials if it seems appropriate in a cover letter or interview, especially if one is relevant to a project I'm applying for. It's clean, concise, and clear and presents a dynamic picture of me as a writer and creator.

This Resume Sucks

Bill Pastry
000 Road Drive
West, TX 77777
555-555-1234
someone@webservice.com

   I am looking for an opportunity to enhance my customer service skills. I enjoy working with people. I am looking for an environment that will allow me to further develop my technology skills.

Personal Information: I have been married to my wife, Joanne, for 18 years. Joanne has taught in Texas ISD for 22 years. We have two sons, George and George. George is a junior in high school and George is in the sixth grade. I enjoy coaching YMCA basketball boys' and girls' leagues and coaching flag football. I also volunteer my time between our two community gardens where produce is given to charitable organizations.

Education:
Graduated from Blah High Academy in 1974. I took a few courses at Southern Blah College.

Work Experience:
- Texas YMCA   Fitness Instructor/Personal Trainer March 2002- Present   Supervisor- Melissa Ewasko
- Tom's Landscaping Self-employed lawn care   1999- present
- Minute Man   Customer Service   July 2000 to March 2001

References:

Miss Smith	Friend for 13 years	444-555-1234
Mr Jones	Customer at YMCA	444-555-1234
Mr Smith	Boy Scouts of America	444-555-1234

This Resume Sucks

Content - This resume is quite possibly the worst resume we have ever seen. Not only don't we know what this person wants to do, he talks more about his wife and kids than he does about himself.

Overall – Mr. Pastry highlights his weaknesses more than his strengths by giving far too much personal information and putting his less than stellar education before work experience.

Job Title - His work experience is so diverse we can't figure out for what job he'd be suited. To further complicate matters; in his objective statement he says he wants to enhance his customer service skills and to further develop his technology skills. Customer service and technology jobs aren't always mutually exclusive, but typically they are on different career paths.

Experience – He includes dates which don't seem to support one career, as he jumps around in the types of jobs he holds. The dates also show that he only works part time at the YMCA and Minute Man because he has been mowing lawns at the same time.

Personal Information - Including this much personal information on a resume shows he has no idea how to present himself. He appears naive and out of touch with business practices. One's resume is never the place to expound on the careers of others as Mr. Pastry does about his wife's employment situation.

Education – It is listed before experience and all it shows is that he graduated from high school and didn't finish college.

References - They do not belong on a resume. When listing references, notate your business relationship (supervisor, manager, associate) rather than friendship.

This Resume Rocks

Customer Service Representative

Bill Pastry
555-555-1234
000 Road Drive
St. Louis, MO 63123
someone@webservice.com

Work Experience
Customer Service Representative
Minute Man

Fitness Instructor/Personal Trainer
Texas YMCA
- Handled all account billing and scheduling

Lawn Care Specialist
Bill's Landscaping
- Earned excellent customer satisfaction ratings

Supporting Experience
Office and Garden Support
Charity Gardens
- Community garden where produce was grown to give to food kitchens

Fundraising Organizer
St. Louis Botanical Gardens

This Resume Rocks

Content – At a glance we now know what he wants to do and how his experience supports that job.

Job Title – We created a job title based on his objective statement and his work experience.

Work Experience
- We eliminated the personal information and objective statement and put work experience before education.
- We changed the order of the work experience to support the job title better.
- Instead of listing who his supervisor was at the Texas YMCA, we added a job description that's not obvious from the job title.
- We rewrote his supporting work experience to make it more relevant.

Dates - Removal of all of the dates eliminated the issue of part-time work and allowed us to put his work experience in the order which best supports the job title.

Education - His education was deleted because it was unimpressive and worked against him.

Design, Formatting, Proofreading
Format – We changed the format totally to make it easier to read and to eliminate the indents.

Fonts – We changed the font from Times New Roman to Futura HV to give his resume a bit bolder look and to make it stand out. When there's a generous amount of white space and you'd like to fill out the page at least visually, a bolder font helps.

This Resume Sucks

Fulls--Real W-- Education:
-- --ed to new ways of thinking in a production e--
Learn-- -- to keep intense schedules, and manage tim--
efficiently. Learned the tools used in the --dustry.(phot--
Shake, Aftereffects).

Goin Postal: (T- Shirt Company)
Created concepts and drawings for this beginning Shirt company.
Designe-- -- ain Going Postal

Mother May I: (Music Company)
Created base concepts, drawings, and 2D Photoshop artwork for
the companies logo, and trademark. Currently contracted to create
The 3D logo for the company.

Customer Serv--
6 yrs Plus expe-- --ing and assisting managers,
clients, and other --veloped excellent ph-- skills, and
office management

Figure 24

This Resume Sucks

Overall
This was an actual resume faxed to our office from a school.
The original resume evidently had graphics on it which turned
to black splotches when sent via fax. A black and white scan
would have the same result. Even if we had liked their
background, we couldn't have called this person because the
contact information was completely unreadable.

Design, Formatting, Proofreading
Design – The shadow under the text makes it look fuzzy on the
fax.

We didn't do a revised version since we couldn't read enough of
this resume to do one.

This Resume Sucks

Resume:

Address:

Phone:
Email:

Education:
: Magic City Campus, Minot ND. - Diploma.
: Full Sail Real World Education, Winter Park FL. - Associates of Science degree in animation.

Projects:
: Business Logo's
- "Mother May I" head designer and artist: Aug 2004 - Sept 2004
: created a traditional logo, and concept art. Also created a 3D version for the web.

- "Going postal" Created the original logo's and character design for this starter-up t-shirt company: Jun 1999 - July 1999

Gear:
: Maya 4.0 - 6.0
: Photoshop 5 - 7
: After Effects
: Shake
: Final Cut Pro

Skills:
: Texturing (Strongest All Around)	3yrs Exp.
: Modeling (Moderate Skills)	1 yr 1/2 Exp.
: Lighting (Moderate)	1 yr 1/2 Exp.
: Compositing (Moderate)	1 yr Exp.
: Rigging (Decent)	1 yr Exp.

Figure 25

This Resume Sucks

Overall

This resume is among the worst we've seen. The hand-written type font is not scannable, hard to read, and leaves an unprofessional impression. The very faint round splotches on the page made us think that we had laid the paper down on an oily surface until we realized that they were an ill-conceived graphic.

Content

Job Title – Lane needs to provide a job title so employers don't have to figure it out. Most won't take the time and they'll just toss his resume into the circular file.

Software – Don't list version numbers because every time a new version comes out your experience looks dated.

Don't rate yourself – Under Skills, Lane elaborates on his abilities by rating them from Decent to Strongest All Around and he states how long he's been using each software. This information makes him appear inexperienced and amateurish. Plus you should never describe yourself as Decent.

Design, Formatting, Proofreading

Contact Information - There is no need to label address, phone and e-mail. An exception is specifying phone numbers as mobile or cell and home. This is a great example of the Duh Factor.

Dates – Judging by the dates, it appears that he has only worked for 3-4 months. This might be true, but you don't want to let others know that you are that new to the work force in such exacting detail. Lane may be a very gifted texture artist, but his career might get side-tracked if he continues to highlight his weaknesses over his strengths. While only verifiable truths belong on one's resume, you are allowed to paint the most positive picture you can of yourself. Once you get hired, you may be required to fill out paperwork where you list each job you've held along with the dates of employment. These dates are being used, not as a screening device, but as a way to verify your background – so be absolutely truthful in filling out all employment paperwork.

Education – It should be listed last, if at all.

This Resume Rocks

Texture/CG Artist
Lane Moran

444-555-1234
mye-mail@awebsite.com

Experience
Logo Designer
Mother May I
- Lead designer and texturer
  - Logo, concept art, and 3D web version.

Logo/Character Designer
Going Postal T-Shirts
- Logos and character design

Software Knowledge
Maya
Photoshop
After Effects
Shake
Final Cut Pro

Education
Full Sail Real World Education
- Associates of Science degree in animation

This Resume Rocks

Overall
When we revised Lane's resume it became quite short. We would recommend that he get more experience or find relevant experience in his background. Offering services for free for friends, school, and family are great ways to gain experience.

Content
Job title - We chose texture artist based on his highest skill level. He may adjust this title to any position for which he feels qualified.

No Dates – With no dates, we are free to arrange Lane's experience to best support the job title.

Experience trumps education – Even though he doesn't have much experience, an employer is still more interested in what he's done on the job than in the class room.

Software version numbers – With the numbers removed the list will stay relevant for as long as someone holds onto his resume. We always suggest inclusion of only the software in which you are extremely proficient. A poor software answer in an interview could cost you an opportunity…and employers do test software knowledge.

Impression - We removed the skills section. We know he can texture because of his title. The other skills seemed too weak and wouldn't help him.

Design, Formatting, Proofreading
Font – Arial and Arial Black fill out the resume and give it a crisp, clean look.

This Resume Sucks

1003 Black Creek Lane
Phone (222) 222-2222
Dallas, TX 77777
E-mail
jgonzalez@yahoo.com

Juan Gonzalez

Education	1994 - 1998	Kingwood High School
	High School Diploma	Dallas, TX

Professional experience

Sept. 2005-March 2006   Blackwater USA
Executive Security Officer
-Provided Personal armed security for FEMA employees and other individuals working on Hurricane Katrina and Rita relief efforts.
-Worked at a disaster relief center distributing supplies to hurricane victims

Jan. 2004-August 2005   Trader Pub
Circulations Supervisor
-Supervised approximately 30 delivery drivers and ensured that over 300 stores received their publications in a timely manner.
-Conducted store audits and wrote reports on productivity of employees
-Provided proposals to multiple new stores with a 95 percent success rate for product placement.

Jan. 2004-June 2004   Microsoft
Technical Support Representative
-Provided technical support for 75 to 100 different customers a day
-Sold service contracts as well repair orders and online website access packages

Dec.1999-Dec.2003   U.S. Marine Corps
Sergeant
-Trained and managed approximately 40 Infantry Marines
-Created weekly training schedules for academic and physical training
-Participated in overseas peace keeping operations
-Veteran of operation Iraqi Freedom - Member of X unit

Awards received   Combat Action Ribbon, Global War on Terrorism Service Medal, Presidential Unit Citation, and Marine Corps Good Conduct Medal

This Resume Sucks

Overall
We have no idea what Juan wants to do or what he's qualified to do because his work experience is poorly organized. By listing high school diploma as the first item on his resume, an immediate negative impression is created in the mind of the recruiter before he has a chance to look at anything else.

Content
Job Titles – Of course he lacks one at the top of his resume so Juan needs to do some research and find something he wants to do and that his work experience supports. Once he decides upon a job title for his resume he needs to organize and edit his work experience so that every job listed either directly or indirectly supports his goal.

Design, Format, Proofreading
Design – This looks like it was created with a resume template from a word processing program. This type of column format does not hold up with OCR.

Contact Information – Way too small! The name is needlessly large; while, the contact info has to be read with a magnifying glass. Okay, I'm exaggerating, but your phone number should not be the smallest thing on the page.

This Resume Rocks

Executive Security Officer
Juan Gonzalez
222-222-2222
jgonzalez@yahoo.com

Decorated Marine Corps Sergeant
Operation Iraqi Freedom Veteran
Highly Trained and Tested Leader

Work Experience
Executive Security Officer
Blackwater USA

- Provided personal armed security for FEMA employees and others working on Hurricane Katrina and Rita relief efforts
- Distributed supplies to hurricane victims at a disaster relief center
- Supervised by Federal Police Department Immigration and Customs Enforcement
- Detained and questioned anyone who had committed a crime or who had acted in a suspicious manner, then wrote a report on the offense

Sergeant
United States Marine Corps
Veteran of Operation Iraqi Freedom

- Trained and managed 40 Marines on a daily basis and occasionally managed 100 or more in a high stress environment
- Created weekly training schedules for academic and physical training
- Served in 3rd Light Armor Reconnaissance Battalion

Training
Certificate in Leadership Training
Advanced Infantry Gunnery Evaluator School
- Graduated in the top 5
- Upon graduation, taught gunnery classes and tested battalion's readiness to perform in combat operations in Iraq.

Commendations
Combat Action Ribbon
Global War on Terrorism Service Medal
Presidential Unit Citation
Marine Corps Good Conduct Medal

This Resume Rocks

Overall

Juan's resume creates a dynamic impression of him as a battle-toughened Marine sergeant who would undoubtedly make an excellent executive security officer. The three branding statements make a powerful, bold, and impressive statement about the kind of person he is and what can be expected of him the future.

* Note: Juan's revised resume fits on one 8.5x11 piece of paper.

Content

Impression - Everything in his resume supports his job title and there is nothing that could leave a negative impression.

Design, Format, Proofreading

Design – Clean, concise, and easy to scan.

Contact information – It is in a prominent place and large enough to read easily.

Format – By listing Juan's commendations one to a line instead of strung together by commas, they are given added prominence and importance.

Appendix 1: Supporting Research

This research supports areas of the text which are marked with asterisks*.

- 1. Companies receive hundreds of resumes.
    - For the last 15 years Dr. James Irvine has been building selection systems for Fortune 500 companies, mom-and-pop operations, and non-profit organizations. They all have one thing in common…when a good company is offering a good job for competitive pay; the resumes will arrive in hordes. It is not uncommon for an organization to receive 100 resumes a week for an entry level position. If the company advertises on the internet, expect 500 to 1,000 resumes a week. For example, Dr. Irvine built a selection system for a golf club company looking for an entry level traveling salesman; they received 125 resumes the first week. A call-center's basic customer service phone position draws in over 200 resumes a week. A basic salaried position in the automotive industry garnered about 250 resumes the first week it was advertised…quadruple that if the internet is involved.
    - According to *U.S. News & World Report*, most Fortune 500 companies receive more than 1,000 unsolicited resumes each week. It is simply impractical and inefficient for an organization to read, track, and file this enormous amount of resumes, so many are utilizing technology to do this for them. The good news is that in the old days of paper resumes, as many as eighty percent of resumes were discarded after only a quick review, at least with scanning technology your

information is stored somewhere. The bad news is that if you don't know how these systems work, human hands may never touch your resume. So learn how to play the game and let this new scanning/database technologies help you to get noticed with a computerized keyword search.

o The number of resumes you can expect to receive will mirror the economic conditions of your area. Research reports that the greatest number of job movements occur when labor markets are strong and unemployment is low (Gerhart, 1990; Spector, 1987). This is common sense. When the economy and labor markets are strong, companies are doing lots of hiring, and when unemployment is low salaries tend to be higher because companies are competing with each other for good people. However, when unemployment is high, there are a lot of people still looking for a job. For higher level positions, resume volumes become greater during times of increased mergers, downsizing, dumb sizing, outsourcing, and off-shoring. This causes highly experienced people to be suddenly searching for a new position, so companies are flooded with tons of resumes. References: Gerhart, B. (1990). Voluntary turnover and alternative job opportunities. *Journal of Applied Psychology*, 75, 467-476.   Spector, P. E. (1997). Job satisfaction Application, assessment, causes, and consequences, Thousand Oaks, CA: Sage Publications. Aon Consulting's Radford Surveys Reports Technology Industry Hiring on the Rise, Layoffs on the Decline in 2004, Business Wire. New York: Aug 30, 2004. pg. 1.

- 2. Recruiters are short on time.
  - If a position receives 600 resumes and each resume is reviewed for 5 minutes, which equals 3,000 minutes just for the first resume review for one position. That equals over 7 working days with no breaks. Thus, recruiters spend little time in their initial review of resumes.
- 3. Most resumes get reviewed in 5-10 seconds.
  - Jobseekernews.com (2003)
- 4. Only a portion of your resume is shown on a monitor at once.
  - Based on a screen size of 1024 x 768, 12 pt text and 14 pt headers.
    - Full-page Word documents have 44 lines of text.
    - The top 27 lines of text are first seen on a full-screen.
    - Minimized windows and large headers will limit the number of lines seen.
- 5. People hire others their age or the age they were when they first held that position.
  - Similar-to-me - We like people that are like us (similar education, history, experiences, hobbies, etc.). Assessors often inflate the rating of individuals they see as similar to themselves (consciously or below their level of conscious awareness). This is natural and normal; we are more comfortable with people that are similar to us than those who are dissimilar. References: Fried, Y, Levi, A. S., Ben-David, H. A., Tiegs, R. B. (1999). Inflation of subordinates' performance ratings: Main and interactive effects of rather negative affectivity, documentation of work behavior, and appraisal visibility, *Journal of Organizational Behavior, 20(4)*, 431-444.

Wayne, S. J., & Liden, R. C. (1995). Effects of impression management on performance ratings: A longitudinal study, *Academy of Management Journal, 38*, 232-260.

o Facts vs. Feelings – consider this information – ("…as little as <u>five percent of</u> the information obtained in a standard interview pertains to skills actually required for a job" *Robert Half, Finding - Hiring, and keeping the Best Employees* According to Robert Half's research, <u>86 percent</u> of interviewers make a decision within the <u>first few minutes</u> of meeting a candidate. *Robert Half, Finding - Hiring, and keeping the Best Employees* "First Impressions" dominate most people's decision-making…70% of all hiring decisions are based on first impressions and personal chemistry. *Lou Adler, Power Hiring - Harvard Business Review.)* What is all this research telling us? People make hiring decisions—face-to-face interviews and resumes—based primarily on intuition, gut-feel, impression, etc. not based on 'fact'. Why is this? Because of our emotional and neurological 'wiring' and our experiences….both nature and nurture.

o Wiring – Why do we often incorrectly process data? Because this is the way your biology and neurology are designed to work. The human brain is not designed to process data in isolation (treat and evaluate each event as a unique and new event). However, the brain is remarkably effective at creating meaning through the comparison and association of new data to all previously stored information. The brain is a connection engine…this can be good, but if not controlled it can also can become a huge liability. Example: Chair → when the eye perceives, and the brain receives data about an object with four legs and a flat surface about 20 inches off the floor, the brain does <u>not</u> start computing all possible scenarios. Is it living? What is it made of? How dense is it? Why is it that color? It first compares it to all stored memories of similar objects attempting to find a match continuously refining the match (chair, table, stand, etc.). Only when no match is found does the brain start 'asking questions' to 'discover' meaning...creating unique meaning is a process of last resort. [Remember the saying, *"Comparison is the thief of joy"*. Humans are naturally wired to process data through comparison.]

o Emotions & Life Experiences – Everyone has feelings and emotions and they will always influence our decisions-making. Your brain is not a general-purpose computer with one unified central processor. It is an assemblage of competing subsystems specialized for particular tasks. Your brain has 'subsystems' or 'routines' running behind the scenes (below conscious awareness) interpreting words through their own emotional processor. Unfortunately, the content and words of the message take a back seat to the flood of other data. Example: If you hated college, or it was an emotionally charged subject with your parents, emotions would flood your brain and influence your thinking every time that subject came up.

o Life experience wires our brains as meticulously as our genes do. Our experiences have a strong influence on what we hear (attune to) and how we interpret (assign meaning to) what we hear. The influence is especially powerful if the experience is tied to a strong emotion. The issue isn't WILL your past influence you, but HOW and WHEN your experiences influence you. Example: Education – if you find out someone has a Harvard degree, that fact alone will have an influence on your perception (belief, opinion) of that person...positively or negatively. Those with a college degree might be impressed (unless they are from a rival school); while for those without a degree it might spark negative emotions.

- 6. People will assume you are the perfect age without contrasting information.
  - o People assume people are 'what they want them to be' because of two major reasons: People want to believe the best about people and people are mentally lazy (or distracted). First, people want to believe the best about people and they want to 'feel' good about themselves and others. Our mind/emotions are designed to seek out a sense of balance, congruence, and equilibrium. As a result, we often 'fill in the blanks' with the information we 'hope' is true or we 'want' to be true. Secondly, the people reading your resume are often mentally lazy or distracted...their brains are operating on autopilot. During the first review of a stack of resumes, they are looking for reasons to 'knock out' a resume; if they don't see something specific, they 'assume' the candidate is qualified. Their primary goal is reduce the hundreds of resumes to a manageable number. In addition, their brain 'wants' to find the 'perfect person' so their search will be over (less work).

This isn't a conscious process, but one that influences behavior anyway. Reference: *Mind Wide Open: Your Brain and the Neuroscience of Everyday Life*, by Steven Johnson, 2004. Simon & Schuster, New York, NY.

- o If you don't make your age apparent, then whoever is considering you for the job is more likely to assume you are the perfect age.

- 7. Age assumption based on graduation date.
  - o When resumes state dates of graduation, recruiters make age assumptions.
  - o Most people graduate college with a Bachelor's degree when they are 22.
  - o Associate degree graduates are more often 19 or 20 years old.
  - o People receiving secondary degrees or degrees later in life will mislead recruiters about their age if their resumes include dates.

- 8. Job-loss excuses leave negative impressions
  - o Why is a job loss—involuntary or voluntary—often viewed as a negative? Recruiters and managers like 'winners' and are attracted to those who are 'successful'. Any job loss will raise questions, spark fears, and fuel uncertainty. Why? Because, someone's past behavior is the best predictor of future behavior (most selection experts believe that the most effective way to reliably predict performance is to assess past performance). The reasoning often goes like this: "If you have lost, there must be a reason, and that reason can not be something good. I don't want to hire that reason here (whatever it is) and I don't have the time to find out the what's and why's." References: Robert Half 1993, *Finding - Hiring, and Keeping the Best Employees*; Lou

Adler, *Power Hiring - Harvard Business Review*; Margaret Dale 1996, *How to be a Better Interviewer*; Michael Mercer 1993 *Hire the Best...and Avoid the Rest*; Richard Deems 1994, *Interviewing: More than a Gut Feeling.*

- 9. People move from job to job.
    - The number of job seekers includes the unemployment and turnover statistics. According to the U.S. Department of Labor Bureau of Labor Statistics (www.bls.gov) March 2005), there were 7.7 million unemployed persons and 1.6 million people 'marginally attached' job seekers. According to the *2004 U.S. Job Recovery and Retention Survey* released November 30, 2004 by the Society for Human Resource Management (SHRM) and CareerJournal.com, 35% of employees said they are actively job searching, and 40% are passively searching. With approximately 133 million people employed in the US (non-farm), which means that 46.5 million people are actively searching and over 53 million are passively searching for a new job.
    - Job mobility in the U.S. work force has become the standard employment pattern in today's workplace. Between 1991 and 1996, the median job tenure for men 25-64 years of age fell by an average of approximately 19 percent, with older workers most affected. Males 55-64 years of age had a 29 percent drop in tenure and males 45-54 years of age, a 25 percent drop (Koretz 1997). Although the job tenure of females remained somewhat constant during this period, this may reflect the increased numbers of women who have entered the work force during these same years rather than stable job tenure patterns.

According to the Bureau of Labor Statistics, 10 percent of the work force switches jobs every year (Henkoff 1996).

o Federal labor statistics show that workers in almost every age group are staying at jobs for a shorter period of time than their counterparts did in the 1980s. For instance, 25 - 34 year olds have held their current jobs for a median of 2.7 years, down from 3 years in 1983.

o Job mobility is even more pronounced in California, where a 1998 Field Poll estimated that nearly half of all workers have held their current job for less than two years. Job hopping is more common and accepted in the high-tech world than in other industries. That's because the tight high-tech labor market, fast pace of technological change and lure of startups with potentially lucrative stock options all create an incentive for skilled workers to move around a lot. Career experts say that today's trend of shorter job tenure has its roots in the downsizing wave of the late 1980s and early 1990s, which shattered many people's expectations of lifetime employment. But other factors have contributed as well:

- A strong economy makes workers more confident that if a job change doesn't work out, they can find something else.
- Many firms have replaced traditional pension plans with more portable 401(k) retirement plans, reducing some of the financial risk of frequent job changes.
- The Internet -- with hundreds of job listings just a keystroke away -- makes it easier than ever before to find out about

other job options.
- The executive recruiter industry has also mushroomed in recent years, so professional-level employees are more likely than before to have someone dangling attractive new jobs in front of them.
  - Reference: *Keeping A Packed Bag At Work: Employees Today are More Apt to Job Hop Than Ever Before* by Ilana DeBare • San Francisco Chronicle.

- 10. Unpaid work is just as valuable, maybe more.
  - Some people devalue unpaid work.
  - Knowledge and experience is gained whether paid or not.
  - Portfolio samples and contacts are gained, whether paid or not.
  - Some people realize that a person willing to work for free or as an intern is the type of person willing to do what it takes to get the job done.

- 11. Reference checks.
  - Most companies now conduct criminal background checks on potential employees. A recent survey of 270 companies, the Society for Human Resource Management reports that 80 percent of companies say they run criminal checks, reference checks, check prior work histories, and many rely on additional background reporting. Approximately 50 percent verify education and check motor vehicle records and 35 percent run credit checks on possible new hires.
  - Technology also has streamlined the process for employers. Legal and financial records are now

maintained electronically and background checks are now easy to acquire online for just a few dollars. The result, companies now check every applicant. For employees with nothing to hide, though, concerns may linger about how all this information is being used by companies. There are protections for workers including the Fair Credit Reporting Act (FCRA) which requires companies to notify applicants if any adverse action occurs based on the data obtained. Likewise, companies must tell applicants what types of checks they conduct and clearly state that any false information could lead to a worker being fired. And the FCRA definition of a consumer report is extremely broad and can include information character, general reputation, personal characteristics, or mode of living.

- o Common types of background checks
  - Criminal Records - search county and federal databases for felony and misdemeanor charges

  - Social Security/Identity Check - Verify that a social security number exists and confirm the appropriate name and addresses of the individual.

  - Employment/Education History - Verify dates of employment, title, salary history. Verify degree earned at a college or university.

  - Motor Vehicle Records - Verify an applicant's driver's license - state of issue, violations, current license status, points, etc.

- Credit Checks - Credit history information through a national credit bureau. Includes names, rating and history, high credit, amount owing, late payments, etc.

o Consider these facts: (www.us.manpower.com)

- 34% of resumes and 73% of job applications contain falsified or embellished information.

- 38% of all employees have been involved in serious acts of dishonesty within the past two years.

- 35% of all business failures (or 36,000 companies per year) can be attributed to employee-related theft.

- Part-time employees are 33% more likely to steal than are full-time employees.

- 29% of employees think everybody steals.
  Reference: *Security Technology & Design*, c 2001 by the Institute of Management & Administration

- Employees who abuse drugs are about 30-35 % less productive than non-users. Reference: National Institute on Drug Abuse as reported in the LA Times, Oct. 2, 2000

- Employed drug abusers cost their employers about twice as much in medical and worker compensation claims as their drug-free coworkers. Reference: National Institute on Drug Abuse in its Workplace Trends, November 5, 1999

- o Also see Appendix 3, Employment Background Checks.

- 12. Online resume verification.
  - o See reference 11 above.
  - o Also see Appendix 3, Employment Background Checks.
- 13. Bi-lingual
  - o The U.S. Census Bureau reports there are over 31 million Latinos in the U.S. (approximately 13% of the U.S. population). Latinos are now the largest ethnic minority group in the U.S. and comprise a significant percentage of the growing middle class. Conservative projections indicate Latinos will comprise 25% of the total U.S. population by the year 2050 (96.5 million) and could be as high as 33% by 2100. This means that the U.S. is experiencing a dramatic increase of bilingual job candidates, as well as a growing bilingual customer base.
- 14. Education may not be necessary on your resume.
  - o Author Mark Simon has landed over 2,500 projects without ever listing his education and he has a degree with two majors. Clients are more concerned with his client list and the samples in his portfolio. In over 20 years, no client has ever asked if he had a degree or if he went to college.
  - o In the creative arts an education does not make you more creative.
  - o If two people apply for the same creative position and one has an education and the other does not,

the one with more experience and better samples will get the job. Education is not a deciding factor.

- o An education, however, can provide opportunities, present new techniques and refine talent.

- 15. Remove software version numbers.
  - o Software constantly updates. Including software version numbers guarantees your resume will become outdated.
  - o Updating software version numbers does not help with resumes already sent out.
  - o Listing operating systems looks like you are padding your resume unless you work in IT or programming.

- 16. Faxes and copy machines turn art into unrecognizable splotches.
  - o Most fax machines stay set to 'Fine' mode. 'Fine' mode is a black and white mode which turns color and gray-scale images and photos into black and white with poor results. Text over an image or photo will mostly be lost in a fax.
  - o If a fax machine is set to 'Photo', an image or photo will be clearer as the fax machine breaks art and photos into the tiny dots you see in a newspaper photo. However, there is no guarantee how your resume will look if it's faxed a second time.
  - o Copy machines set on 'Auto' or 'Standard' will also turn art and photos into black and white splotches.

- 17. File Name.
  - o If you simply title your resume file 'resume.doc', the recruiter's computer will assign your resume a new title in numerical order along with all the

other 'resume.doc' files they have received. Example: 'resume32991.doc'.

- o Including your name and job title in the file name helps recruiters find and organize your resume. Jobseekernews.com weekly tips, June 05, 2003.

- 18. Resumes get passed along by fax and paper copies.
  - o Finding a reliable person is more important to an employer than finding the perfect person. When small companies look for employees, they ask friends for suggestions. Those friends may fax or make copies of resumes to send to the employer. You will have little control over what happens to your resume, other than to anticipate this and to properly prepare your resume.

- 19. OCR, Optical Character Recognition.
  - o See Appendix 2, The Electronic Resume.

- 20. Digitized versions of resumes.
  - o Most companies have their own 'records retention policy' for both solicited (advertised) and unsolicited resumes (this varies by the size of the organization and government requirements). A common practice is to retain electronic copies of resumes for 1 year, unsolicited resumes for 1 year, and for solicited resumes the 'official/original' copy is retained for 2 years

- 21. Back-up version of your resume on the internet.
  - o The internet offers a way for you to access your resume, cover letter, and any other important information regardless of where you may be.
  - o If you are traveling and looking for a job, you may need to access certain files.
  - o Free e-mail accounts on Yahoo.com and MSN.com, among others, are great places to save your resumes and other files. You can e-mail an

attachment to yourself and retrieve it at any time from any place with an internet connection.

- 22. Fancy fonts on your resume may not scan properly.
  - o OCR, Optical Character Recognition programs are designed to read specific shapes of letters. Some fancy fonts may cause the program to misread some letters turning them into symbols and misspellings. Fine lines in some fonts may not be seen on some scans and further disrupt the quality of the character recognition.
- 23. Use of key words.
  - o Many employers are now using relational database technology to store and search resumes. The technology works like this…a computer searches the database and evaluates each resume using keywords. Keywords are words and phrases that highlight technical and professional areas of expertise, industry-related jargon, achievements, projects, job titles, etc. Sometimes these keyword searches are extremely sophisticated (like 10 line-long Boolean phrases), and other times they are ultra-simplistic (single word).

    Even if you have all of the experience and skills required, but your resume doesn't contain the desired keyword, your resume could be skipped by the computer. The bottom line: key words can make you or break you.

    Here a few basic principles for using keywords in your resume:
    - A great source of keywords is the actual job listing, which is likely to contain many, if not all, of the keywords that an employer will use to search the resume database. Read the job description for

"must have" skills. These qualifications will give you an idea of what a recruiter will be searching on. They may also help you prioritize or better understand what keywords would be pertinent to your qualifications. Companies often use different terminology from what you might use; the job description/ad can help you break the code.

- Compare the keywords used in your "targeted" job with the keywords used in the "next level higher" job. The new or added words in the "higher" level job are the most important to use if you expect to get a higher pay rate.

- Include plenty of keyword nouns and noun phrases throughout your resume. If you have a "Summary of Qualifications" section at the beginning of your resume, try not to repeat verbatim the contents of this section.

- If you are applying for technical positions, you can list your skills, separating each noun or phrase by a comma.

- In some fields, a simple list of skills does not sufficiently describe the job seeker's background. Where appropriate, include accomplishments, as well, but be sure to include enough keywords to satisfy the computer searches.

- Don't stress over the phrasing of the "soft skills." It is rare that a search is done on "creative problem solver."

- Identify the key "values" of the company you are targeting. These values can generally be found either listed separately (company values) on the firms Web page or in the firm's "mission" statement.
- Next look for any key "competencies" that the firm lists on its Web page. These can either be competencies of the firm or competencies that are expected for all employees.
- Action verbs speak volumes! In addition to "hard skills," many recruiters also search on "action verbs" that may tell more about the applicant's experience. These words may include "design*," "develop*,"   "present*,"   "lead," "manage*," or "test*." You get the idea.

o   See Appendix 4, Key Words For Resume and Cover Letter Construction.

o   Also see Appendix 2, The Electronic Resume

- 24. Proofreading.

o   Further suggestions for accurate proofreading may be found in the *Gregg Reference Manual* by William A. Sabin, published by McGraw-Hill.

Appendix 2: The Electronic Resume

According to *U.S. News & World Report*, most Fortune 500 companies receive more than 1,000 unsolicited resumes each week. It is simply impractical and inefficient for an organization to read, track, and file this enormous amount of resumes, so many are utilizing technology to do this for them. The good news is that in the old days of paper resumes, as many as eighty percent of resumes were discarded after only a quick review, at least with scanning technology your information is stored somewhere. The bad news is that if you don't know how these systems work, human hands may never touch your resume. So learn how to play the game and let this new scanning/database technology to help you get noticed with a computerized keyword search.

The Technology
As technology has progressed, it has greatly affected resume writing and job searching. As the number of job applicants increases each year, organizations are turning to technology— scanning and Optical Character Recognition (OCR) software— to: 1) reduce the amount of physical handling, filing, and storage of paper resumes, and 2) increase the organization's ability to search for specific job skills and abilities. This adds another element to the job search game, because resumes written for the human eye are different than those written for the "digital eye." Like a human, computers scan the resume for "keywords," but they have a limited ability to recognize or interpret. A person scanning your resume has the ability to recognize, interpret, and appreciate fancy formatting, columns, and fonts. Not so with a computer; they want things simple. The challenge – How do I make my resume stand out in a database of millions?

Understanding the Technology

What happens when you create a beautiful paper resume and then mail or fax it to a company that scans that resume into a computerized database? When an organization utilizes a computerized tracking system, your resume is transferred from paper to binary information to be stored in the computer. The digitized resume is reformatted to 'populate' specific fields the company believes are important. At this point, you lose some control over the content of your resume and lose complete control over the formatting. The scanner utilizes software called Optical Character Recognition (OCR) designed to detect and examine the ink on the page and translates those shapes into letters. The software then matches patterns of letters (keywords) with those programmed into its memory.

Keywords

The primary purpose of the resume database software is to create a prioritized list of applicants from most qualified to least qualified. Resume databases are programmed to search for and identify the keywords that define the important knowledge, skills, and abilities required by the job. The number of "hits" a resume has (match between desired keywords and found keywords), determines if and where your name will appear on the prioritized list of applicants. These systems are typically programmed to only "recommend" resumes that contain a certain number of "hits." Some keywords also serve as "knockout" criteria…if there isn't a hit, the resume is not even considered. For example, if a position calls for "CPA" or a "College Degree" and the scanning software does not find it, the resume may stay buried in a database somewhere.

Some resume scanning systems can be very sophisticated. Resumix is one of the most widely used systems utilizing over 10 million key words and 120,000 decision rules to extrapolate information for placement in the database. This type of sophisticated artificial intelligence enables a hiring manager to customize the keyword search to each specific job opening. One of the best places to find the relevant keywords is from the job ad itself. Almost every noun in the job posting or ad, and many key adjectives, are keywords. Make a list of the key words you believe are important for the job you are pursuing, and make sure that you use those words somewhere in your resume. It is impossible to list all of the possible keywords that your job would require, but the key is to match the job advertisement's verbiage closely or exactly.

Changing Priorities – nouns not action verbs

In today's world of e-mailed and scannable resumes, it is critical that you know the keywords of your job, company, and industry and incorporate them into your resume. Keywords are the nouns or short phrases that describe your experience, education, or skills that are used by scanning and database programs to sort candidates. They are the essential knowledge, skills, and abilities required to do the job. They can be concrete descriptions (credit analyst, supervisor, project management, etc.), software programs (C++, UNIX, etc.), universities (Harvard, SMU, etc.), certifications (MBA, CPA, etc.), or less specific criteria (call-center, customer service, collections, etc.). Keywords are utilized to screen out or narrow down the hundreds or thousands of resumes to a manageable number of 'most qualified' or 'ideal' candidates.

Acronyms and abbreviations can both hurt you or help you depending on how you use them. If the scanning or OCS software is searching for a keyword that is an abbreviation that you spelled out, it may ignore it; and likewise, if the system is looking for something spelled out and you abbreviate it (Visual Basic vs. VB), the system may ignore it.

Advantage

You can use this New World of electronic resumes to your advantage. If you know the rules of the new game better than your competition—everyone else applying for your job—the electronic format can become one of your greatest assets. One of the greatest advantages of electronic résumé's is that companies rarely limit resume length. You can include as much information and as many keywords as you like. However, be careful. If someone prints out your resume and reads it, make sure the most important information is up front and don't include irrelevant information. Build the resume primarily for the computer, but always keep the human in mind.

Common Pitfalls
Here are some of the common pitfalls that may cause a good resume to scan poorly.

- Computer systems have an easier time picking out nouns than verbs. Scannable resumes must be written using the nouns which describe the applicant's qualifications, rather than with traditional action verbs.
- Fancy type style – highly decorative style are difficult or impossible for many OCR software systems to recognize. Often, these systems ignore fancy fonts or they misinterpret letters resulting in misspelled words (i.e. bmkkeepmg). Avoid using decorative fonts (Script, Calligrapher, etc.) and stick with the more simple Serif Fonts (Times Roman, Bookman, etc.), or the very simple Sans Serif Fonts (Arial, Tahoma, Helvetica, etc.).
- Font size for body text should not be smaller than 9 points and not larger that 12 points.
- Avoid using underlining. If you use underlining on your resume, make sure the line does not touch the descenders or 'tails' on letters (g, j, p, q, y, etc.), because scanners have a difficult time distinguishing the shapes of letters when they overlap each other or a line.
- Italics are typically not a problem for the sophisticated systems like Resumix and SmartSearch2 as long as the letters do not overlap or touch.

- Avoid indention. Make sure that every line starts on the left margin to avoid confusing the scanner and OCS software.
- Bullets are another cause for problems, especially if they are fancy or hollow bullets. If they are recognized at all, often they are interpreted as the letter "o". To avoid this, only use simple solid bullets.
- Special characters (%, &, $, (), [], etc.) can often cause problems for scanners and software. Less-sophisticated systems even have problems with **boldface**.
- Rely on white space to separate sections instead of lines. Scanners 'read' the contrast between ink and paper and do better with simple contrasts. Vertical lines are often are interpreted as letters (l, t, etc), horizontal lines are typically ignored, and doted lines (.......) cause significant problems.
- Scanners assume that the document is text written continuously from left to right across the entire page, so be careful when using columns. OCR software has difficulty recognizing columns and differentiating where one sentence begins and another ends. Usually information set in columns becomes garbage.
- Your goal is to develop a clean, high-contrast resume, so only use high quality white paper and a good printer. Scanners assume your resume will be printed on standard sized 8½ X 11 papers. If you are mailing a resume, mail it in a 9 X 12 standard envelope, because folding the resume will often cause the ink to crack, peal or flake and the scanner/OCR will misread or misinterpret information.
- Summit your resume in the format requested. Typically organizations prefer ASCII, Word, RTF, PDF, or HTML formats. Most organizations prefer MS Word, but if no format is designated send it in a couple different formats.

Don't include your resume as an attachment only. Instead, include your cover letter and resume as part of your e-mail message.

Appendix 3: Employment Background Checks: A Jobseeker's Guide

Often, the decision to make a job offer depends on the information revealed during the background check. More and more job applicants, candidates for promotion, and volunteers are being asked to submit to background checks. For many jobs, screening is required by federal/state law or required by insurance carriers. Employers are concerned with protecting themselves and their customers, while applicants and employees are concerned with protecting their privacy rights. Applicants often worry that a company might dig into areas that have nothing to do with the job.

This section clarifies the *why* and *how* of background checks and explains your rights under the Fair Credit Reporting Act. Although every state and organization has different requirements and practices, this will provide a basic overview. For specifics, contact your local employment representative or an employment lawyer.

Part 1. Why Does an Employer Conduct a Background Check?

Employers often conduct background checks of applicants and current workers for varied reasons. The information the employer collects will be based on job and organizational requirements. The most common reasons for employment screening include:

- **Negligent hiring** - Lawsuits of all kinds are on the rise. Often employers are held liable if an employee's actions hurt employees, vendors, or customers. A poor hiring decision can cost the company millions in damages and destroy the companies brand image.

- **Current events - For** North America, the world has changed. Oklahoma City, the events of September 11th, and incidence of school violence have caused an increase in employment screening. Everyone is being more careful today.

- **Child abuse and child abductions** – Recent events have resulted in almost every state passing laws that require criminal background checks for almost anyone who works with children.

- **False or inflated information** – Recent research has highlighted a growing epidemic of applicants falsifying documents. Recent news reports indicate that as much as 40% of all job applications and resumes include some false or inflated data. As a result, it is rare that any employers will accept someone's word as truth.

- **Federal and state laws** – For many jobs, federal and state laws require background checks. Many state and federal government jobs require extensive investigations for a security clearance, or financial investigation for key positions in accounting, finance, audit, etc.

- **Computer technology** - Technology itself is a major reason for the increase in employment screening. What use to be a tedious, difficult and expensive process has become fast, easy, and cheap. With the availability of computer databases of personal data, the number of third party companies has exploded making it painless for employers to order extensive background checks.

Part 2. What Can be Included in a Background Check?

Background checks range from a verifying the applicant's Social Security number, to credit checks, criminal checks, educational verification, or detailed interviews with past employers, neighbors, and acquaintances. Background checks may include almost anything that is accessible from public records.

Driving records	Vehicle registration	Credit records	Criminal records
Social Security no.	Education records	Court records	Workers' compensation
Bankruptcy	Character references	Neighbor interviews	Medical records
Property ownership	Military records	State licensing records	Drug test records
Past employers	Personal references	Incarceration records	Sex offender lists

Part 3. What Can't Be Included in a Background Check?

The Federal Fair Credit Reporting Act (FCRA) sets the national standards for what an employer can and cannot do with external inquiries. Under the FCRA, a background check report is called a "consumer report" or a "consumer investigative report." There are constant changes to the FCRA, so find out the latest rulings in your state. For example, in many states felony convictions can now be reportable indefinitely; not in California. Current guidelines of the FCRA indicate an employer *should not* receive information on:

- Civil suits, civil judgments, and records of arrest, from date of entry, after seven years.

- Bankruptcies after 10 years.

- Paid tax liens after seven years.

- Accounts placed for collection after seven years.

- Any other negative information (except criminal convictions) after seven years.

Arrest & Criminal history. Although arrest record information is public record, most companies inquire only about convictions. The use of criminal histories also depends on individual state law. However, both applicants and employers need to remember, that any information offered to the public is not always accurate or up-to-date. Mistakes happen often caused by identity theft, similar names, and simple clerical errors. As with credit reporting, it is the applicant's job to obtain a copy of a background check and make sure everything is accurate and updated.

Workers' compensation claims. In most states, workers' compensation claims are part of the public record. Currently, the Americans with Disabilities Act states that employers cannot use medical information or any workers' compensation claims to discriminate against an applicant...but if the information is available, who knows how it is being used.

Bankruptcy. All bankruptcies are part of the public record and easy to find. In most states, employers are not allowed to discriminate against applicants because they have filed for bankruptcy, but many financial positions/companies will not consider anyone with a less than 'ideal' credit history.

Are any records confidential?

The Fair Credit Reporting Act requires that employers obtain a written release (i.e. your permission) before conducting background checks. For example, most schools will not release **education records** without authorization, but some will provide basic data (name, address, attendance dates, and degrees earned) without written permission. **Military service records** are confidential and can only be released with authorization under very specific circumstances. However, permission is not required to obtain name, rank, salary, duty assignments, and duty status. **Medical records** are highly confidential. If a specific job requires a physical examination, this is typically only done after the job offer is made and only concerning aspects considered job relevant.

Past Employers: What is someone allowed to say about me?

Most companies only confirm dates of employment, final salary, and job title. Many states have laws specifically prohibiting employers from intentionally interfering with former employees' attempts to find jobs by giving out false or misleading references. However, a former employer can provide any factual information about your performance. Most state laws provide the employee the opportunity to review their personnel files and make copies of any signed documents.

Appendix 4, Key Words for Resume and Cover Letter Construction

Action Verbs

accelerated	activated	adapted	administered	analyzed
approved	assisted	completed	conceived	conducted
controlled	coordinated	created	delegated	developed
directed	eliminated	established	evaluated	expanded
expedited	experienced	expanded	facilitated	generated
implemented	improved	increased	influenced	initiated
interpreted	launched	lead	lectured	maintained
managed	mastered	motivated	organized	originated
participated	performed	pinpointed	planned	prepared
programmed	proposed	proved	recommended	reduced
reinforced	revamped	reviewed	revised	scheduled
set-up	simplified	solved	streamlined	structured
supervised	supported	taught	trained	worked
removed	reorganized	repeated	responsible	

Active Words

accurately	active	adaptable	adept	aggressive
alert	ambitious	analytical	assertive	astute
attentive	aware	broad-minded	challenging	competent
conscientious	consistent	constructive	contributor	creative
dependable	determined	diplomatic	disciplined	discreet
diverse	dynamic	easily	economical	efficient
energetic	enterprising	enthusiastic	exceptional	experienced
expertise	extensively	extroverted	facilitator	fair
forceful	foresight	high-level	honest	imaginative
independent	initiative	innovative	instrumental	insightful
leading	logical	loyal	mature	methodical
objective	optimistic	participated	perceptive	personable
pioneering	pleasant	positive	practical	productive
readily	realistic	reliable	repeatedly	resourceful
responsible	responsive	self-reliant	sensitive	sincere
sophisticated	strongly	systematic	tactful	talented
unique	versatile	vigorous	will travel	will relocate

Meet the Resume Rebels

Mark Simon

Everything in Mark's life revolves around telling stories. As a pitch expert and co-owner of Sell Your TV Concept Now, Inc., he works with content creators to craft pitches which will enthrall potential buyers. Mark has been hired by Disney, Nickelodeon, The Golf Channel, HSN and other networks to help pitch in-house productions. He has also developed and pitched IP created with Jeanne Simon and inked 40+ production and distribution deals.

As a storyboard artist and owner of Storyboards & Animatics, Inc, he teams up with film and TV directors to bring their visions and scripts to life. He is best known for his work as the storyboard artist on *The Walking Dead, Dynasty, Miracle Workers, Cipher,* and dozens of feature films for Universal, Fox, Warner Bros. and most recently Jon Favreau.

Mark is a 30-year veteran producer and director for live-action and animation and has piled up an impressive 5,000 production credits.

As much as Mark pushes his storytelling, he also pushes himself to excel in digital storyboarding. He won a 2012 Prime Time Engineering Emmy for his work with the Toon Boom software team behind Storyboard Pro. He was also inducted into the DAVE School (Digital Animation & Visual Effects School) Hall of Fame.

Mark is not only a storyboard artist, he is an in-demand instructor and has produced multiple training courses for LinkedIn Learning, formerly known as Lynda.com.

Books are another chapter in Mark's story. He has penned ten best-selling industry texts on storyboarding, animation, and several photographic artist reference books.

He has traveled the world telling stories and sharing his expertise as a lecturer at major pitch conferences, entertainment industry trade schools, and universities.

As the father of identical twin young men, he has filled their hearts and minds with stories about how to live a life doing what you love.

The answer to the question you have right now is NO... he doesn't get much sleep.

His storyboard and animation clients include: The Walking Dead, Disney, Universal, Viacom, Sony, HBO, Nickelodeon, FOX, Starz, Steven Spielberg, USA Networks, ABC Television and many others. He was the animation producer of Universal's *How High 2*, Fox's *Tooth Fairy 2* starring Larry the Cable Guy and Universal's 2014 release of *Little Rascals*.

You can reach Mark at MarkSimonBooks@yahoo.com

Jeanne Pappas Simon

Jeanne is a co-writer of *Your Resume Sucks!*

Jeanne has been a producer, writer, and content creator in the entertainment industry for over 25 years. She has been hired for hundreds of jobs on the strength of her resume. Jeanne's work as a producer for over 400 shows such as Nickelodeon's *Clarissa Explains It All, Roundhouse, International Blue's Clues, Gullah Gullah Island, Allegra's Window,* Cartoon Network's *Carrot Top's A.M. Mayhem,* and TNN's *Roller Jam* put her in a position to review hundreds of resumes as she crewed shows.

Her more creative endeavors have been successful as well. The Gen X network she co-developed and co-wrote for Turner Broadcasting was approved by Scott Sassa. She won two international awards for *The Winkles,* an animated short she created and wrote for pre-schoolers. She also co-wrote and co-developed the award-winning animated shorts *Suburban Cinderella* and *Timmy's Lessons in Nature which* won the Grand Prize in Nicktoons inaugural animation festival.

Jeanne was also named one of the Top 40 Under 40 business people in Central Florida for her achievements in business and her contributions to the community.

Jeanne now runs SellYourTvConceptNow.com, helping people to sell their TV show ideas.

Dr. James Elliot McPhee Irvine, D.M.

Dr. Jim Irvine is a co-author of *Your Resume Sucks!* and currently works for Nissan North America. He's designed many of the internal and external selection systems currently in use. He has a thorough understanding of resumes and the selection process. Last year alone, he was involved in filling hundreds of positions, reviewing thousands of resumes, and counseling employees on how to get promoted. As a result, he knows which resumes gets noticed and which ones get ignored.

Likewise, Jim is responsible for designing and delivering many training programs focused on the selection, leadership, and employee motivation. Training classes include: *Your Resume: The key to getting noticed; Conducting Behavioral Interviews: Differentiating Between Superior and Average Performers; Situational Interviewing: Diagnosing Competence & Commitment; Nailing the Interview: Secrets of the Behavioral Interview; How to Get the Promotion You've Always Wanted: Strategies for Networking, resumes, interviewing; Leveraging Your Strengths: 'Selling' your Knowledge, Skills, and Abilities;* **SHIFT_***Performance: Leading the Performance Challenge; The One Minute Motivator: Motivation, Performance, and Profitability; Flack Catching: Dealing with Customer complaints; Mentoring and Coaching Your Employees: Getting Your Employees that Next Promotion; Coaching for Customer Loyalty;* and *Utilizing*

Employee Teams to Drive Change.

Before working for Nissan, Jim worked as a HR/Management consultant with clients such as Atmos Energy, Citizens Telecom, G.E. Aircraft, Lennox, Memorex-Telex, Midas, SeaLand/CSX Lines, Texas Instruments, TransAmerica, Trinity Industries, etc. Jim holds undergraduate and graduate degrees in Business and Psychology and Doctorate of Management in Organizational Leadership.

For the last 25 years - as a researcher, writer, speaker, and consultant - Jim has been sharing the message that an organization's people are the primary determiner of organizational success. As a result, his research has focused on identifying the key elements that differentiate average performers from superior performers and developing selection and development systems based on those differentiating elements.

What others have to say about
Jim Irvine's books and lectures:

"Best class I've ever attended! Very timely practical techniques that can be implemented."

"Excellent—very engaging training and solid "take-aways" to apply right away. Best training I've been in!"

"Great training material. Very useful and facilitator had high energy and knowledge of the subject."

"I think the training was very good and opened my eyes to where I was lacking as a manager."

"This Situations Leadership model is realistic—practical and I'm looking forward to using it."

"Great tool for helping me become a stronger more effective manager."

"This training workshop, SHIFT_Performance - Situational Leadership® II, is providing Nissan exactly what we need, exactly when we need it. In my operation, these leadership workshops have set a new standard for leadership behavior, created new business language—a language of leadership—and provided us a more effective method/approach for leading others. In my 15 years with Nissan, I have never seen any training program create the level of enthusiasm that this one has in such a short amount of time. In my role, I am primarily focused on bottom-line results and operational performance. This program has equipped my managers with the practical skills needed to deliver bottom-line results while simultaneously increasing employee engagement, commitment and ultimately performance. Without a doubt, this has been a great investment of management time and Nissan resources."

Nissan Operations Executive

Thanks for reading. If you enjoyed this book, please leave a review on Amazon.com.

Mark Simon's Other Books

You can find more details on Mark's books and lectures and all sorts of interesting things about him at www.MarkSimonBooks.com

Storyboards: Motion In Art, 3rd Edition

The bible of the industry, used at schools and studios around the world. Used by beginners and seasoned pros alike. Covers every aspect of storyboarding from the art of the craft, to the business of boarding, pricing, how to get started, tricks of the trade, interviews, exercises and over 1,000 samples. No other book on storyboarding comes close to this one.

Your Resume Sucks!

Everything you thought you knew about resumes is WRONG! Your resume needs to work for YOU, not the employer. Resume writing secrets revealed through an entertaining story. Before and after examples of resumes are included.

Facial Expressions

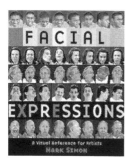

Facial Expressions is a series of photographic reference books for artists of all styles. The first in the series, featuring adults ages 20-83, includes over 3,200 photos of 50 models. Other galleries included feature kissing, phonemes, hats and headgear, skull and more.

Facial Expressions – Babies to Teens
The follow-up print book to the best-selling Facial Expressions series, Babies to Teens, features photos of 63 models ranging from 3 weeks old to 19 years old. Other galleries include skulls, hats, phonemes, age progression and more.

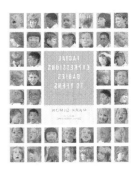

Mind Your Art & Animation Business

Fun articles about serious business. Earn more money in your creative business. Covers all creative endeavors. Based on Mark's hugely popular articles, Mind Your Business, as seen in Animation Magazine and Animation World Network (AWN).

DIY TV Pitch Kit
Do you have a TV concept to sell...or want to someday? Imagine how much faster you could sell your idea for a TV show if you had a step-by-step, easy as 1-2-3, course on everything you need to do

to get your show ready to pitch and info on how to get those coveted pitch meetings.

Mark Simon's Live Talks

http://www.marksimonbooks.com/lectures/

Mark has spoken at events around the world on topics ranging from business and promotion to storyboarding and animation to pitching and selling.

Here is a brief description of a few of his talks.

How I Got More Than $3 Million In Free Publicity

Mark Simon, entertainment industry expert, gets thousands of dollars in free publicity every month. Discover his secrets and increase the exposure for your property.

Start At The Top

Inspiring stories from Simon's book of the same title, and a few extras stories that he held back.

Pitch Like A Pro

The best idea won't sell without a great pitch. Learn what is needed in a great pitch and what to avoid.

Storyboarding

Discover the secrets to storyboarding from the Godfather of Storyboarding, Mark Simon.

Land More Freelance Jobs

Job Search MYTHS Exposed!

E-mailing resumes WILL NOT land you freelance gigs.

Mark Simon's LinkedIn Learning Courses

https://lnkd.in/marksimon

Course – Toon Boom Storyboard Pro Essential Training

Course – 3D Storyboarding with Storyboard Pro

Course – Wacom Tablet: Customizing ExpressKeys

Course – Voice-Over for Video and Animation

Course – Using Character Animator in Production

Made in the USA
San Bernardino, CA
23 January 2020

63542434R00093